# The R. Crumb Coffee Table Art Book

REALLY, DAHLING, IF IT'S NOT EXPENSIVE, IT'S NOT AHT!

OH SHUT UP, DAHLING! ONE MUSTN'T BE SO OB-VIOUS!

R. CRUMB '97

## Edited & Designed by Peter Poplaski

a Kitchen Sink Press book
for
BLOOMSBURY

First published in Great Britain 1997
Bloomsbury Publishing Plc, 38 Soho Square, London W1V 5DF

This paperback edition first published 1998
First published in the United States by Little, Brown and Company
Published simultaneously in Canada by Little, Brown & Company (Canada) Limited

A CIP catalogue record for this book
is available from the British Library.

ISBN 0 7475 3816 6

10 9 8 7 6 5 4 3 2 1

IM

Printed in Hong Kong

# Contents

# FULMINATIONS:

## I RARELY EVER GET COHESIVE IDEAS.

# "MY EARLIEST MEMORY OF COMIC BOOKS IS THE WAY THEY SMELLED!"

**B**EFORE **I** GOT GLASSES, I COULDN'T SEE WELL. BUT I REMEMBER LOOKING AT THE COVERS OF DISNEY COMICS, AND I WAS FASCINATED BY THE WHITE ROUND HEADS OF DONALD DUCK AND HIS NEPHEWS OR MICKEY MOUSE WITH HIS BLACK EARS. THOSE THINGS WERE INSTANTLY RECOGNIZABLE!

WHEN I WAS A KID, I LIKED TO DRAW...BUT MY BROTHER CHARLES FORCED ME TO DRAW COMICS! IF I DIDN'T DRAW COMICS, I WAS A WORTHLESS HUMAN BEING. SO I DREW THEM. I MADE THEM UP ON THE SPOT AS I WENT ALONG. IT WAS TEDIOUS LABOR, SO I WORKED FAST TO GET IT OVER WITH. I DREW YEARS AND YEARS OF *BROMBO THE PANDA* COMICS THAT WERE REALLY UNINSPIRED, BUT I HAD TO TURN THEM OUT ON A MONTHLY SCHEDULE ... GET THEM COMICS OUT! IT WAS OBLIGATORY! WITHOUT MY BROTHER CHARLES FORCING ME TO DRAW COMICS, TODAY I WOULD BE A COMMERCIAL ILLUSTRATOR SIGNING MY WORK "BOB DENNIS."

**U**SUALLY WE DREW ON THE FLOOR. WE HUNCHED DOWN, WE HAD AN OLD COLORING BOOK THAT WE WOULD LEAN ON FOR A DRAWING BOARD AND OUR PENCILS AND CRAYONS IN COFFEE CANS NEXT TO US. OFTEN AS LITTLE KIDS, WE WOULD DRAW TOGETHER ON THE FLOOR OF THE BEDROOM. IT WAS HARD TO GET THE OTHER KIDS INTO DRAWING COMICS. MAXON COULDN'T DRAW AT ALL WHEN WE WERE KIDS, AND SANDRA TRIED TO DO COMICS FOR A WHILE, BUT SHE WAS TOO LAZY. SHE HAD A CHARACTER CALLED "BLACK EYED SUSAN," WHO WAS A GIRL FLOWER WITH A FACE. CHARLES LIKED "GHOSTING" *SANDRA CRUMB'S BLACK EYED SUSAN* COMICS BECAUSE IT WAS LIKE THE DISNEY COMICS. IT WAS KIND OF FUN TO PRETEND YOU WERE IN THE REAL COMICS INDUSTRY. AND I WOULD SOMETIMES "GHOST" *CHARLES CRUMB'S FUZZY THE BUNNY* FOR HIM. WE EVEN HAD SUBSCRIPTION ADS ON THE BACK COVER.

**W**HEN HE WAS A KID, CHARLES WAS OBSESSED WITH COMIC BOOKS AND WITH THE STORY ELEMENT OF COMIC BOOKS. IT USED TO AMAZE ME! I REMEMBER WE WOULD BE LYING IN BED AT NIGHT AND I'D ASK HIM IF HE WAS AWAKE, AND HE'D SAY, "YEAH."

"WELL, WHAT ARE YOU THINKING ABOUT?"

**H**E'D SAY, "OH, I'M JUST THINKING ABOUT A PLOT FOR A STORY." I USED TO THINK, "JEEZIZ, I WISH I COULD DO THAT!" I ALWAYS FELT INADEQUATE BECAUSE I NEVER LAY IN BED THINKING UP PLOTS FOR STORIES. I JUST DID IT AND GOT IT OVER WITH AS FAST AS I COULD. I WAS MUCH MORE INTERESTED IN DRAWING. I LIKED DRAWING CARS AND BUILDINGS FROM PHOTOGRAPHS... I LIKED DOING THE COLOR, BUT CHARLES DIDN'T. HE NEVER TRIED DRAWING MUCH OUTSIDE OF THOSE ANIMATED CARTOON CHARACTERS! HE JUST WASN'T INTERESTED IN ANYTHING ELSE.

**T**HE COMICS WE LOOKED AT AS KIDS WERE ALL FUNNY ANIMAL COMICS ... *DONALD DUCK* ... *ANDY PANDA*. CHARLES LIKED *MIGHTY MOUSE* AND *HECKLE AND JECKLE* AND THEN *LITTLE LULU*, WHICH WERE FIRST BROUGHT HOME FOR MY OLDER SISTER CAROL. IT WAS CONSIDERED A GIRLS' COMIC, I GUESS.

**B**Y THE AGE OF 7 OR 8, WE HAD BEGUN DRAWING OUR OWN COMICS, AND THAT COMPELLED US TO STUDY COMICS MUCH MORE CAREFULLY, MUCH MORE CLOSELY. THEN THE GOOD STUFF STARTED TO SHINE OUT! WE WERE CONNOISSEURS BY AGE 11. BY THEN IT WAS OBVIOUS TO US THAT MOST COMICS WERE HACKED-OUT CRAP. BORING. STUPID. OUTSIDE OF THE REALLY GOOD STORYTELLERS LIKE CARL BARKS AND JOHN STANLEY, THERE WERE ONLY A FEW COMICS THAT ATTRACTED US. I LIKED *SUPERDUCK*, WHICH WAS COMPLETELY WACKO AND STILL STRIKES ME AS IMAGINATIVE AND FUNNY WHEN I LOOK AT IT TODAY. I LIKED *NANCY*. I REMEMBER READING *NANCY* WHILE SITTING ON THE TOILET. BUT AROUND OUR HOUSE, A COPY OF THE DECEMBER 1948 ISSUE OF *WALT DISNEY'S COMICS AND STORIES* WAS ALWAYS LYING AROUND! I DON'T KNOW WHERE IT CAME FROM ... IT WAS LIKE A FIXTURE! AS A KID, I READ THIS COMIC OVER AND OVER! WHEN I WAS 9 YEARS OLD, I HAND-COPIED THE GREAT BARKS STORY ABOUT DONALD AND HIS NEPHEWS GOING ON A QUIZ SHOW. OF COURSE, I CHANGED THE DUCKS INTO OUR CHARACTERS!

*above*, from "Brombo the Panda," *Weirdo* no. 2, 1981; *opposite*, drawing for *People Magazine*, 1985; *center*, panel by Charles Crumb from "Treasure Island Days," 1961

Comics from R. Crumb's collection. *opposite, Little Lulu* no. 110, 1946; *clockwise from right, Pogo Possum* no. 4, 1951; *Paul Terry's Comics* no. 98, 1952; *Krazy Life Hilarious Comics* no. 1, 1945; *Krazy Komics* no. 4, 1942; *Animal Comics* no. 14, 1944

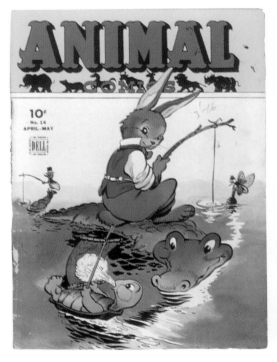

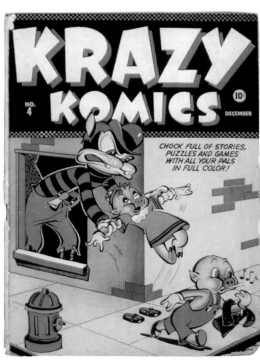

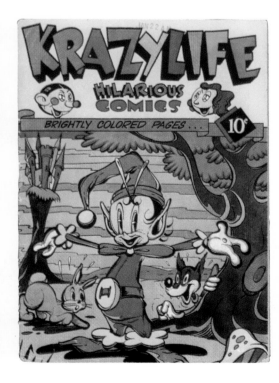

My brother Charles drew this Fuzzy the Bunny comic in December '52. I used to read it over and over again when I was a kid, so much so that it became iconographic to me. This Fuzzy the Bunny thing was just a rambling adventure. Years later, I was burned out—I didn't have any ideas, and when I was required to do a story for *Zap* 5, I kind of copied Charles' story in my style of 1970.

"The Adventures of Fuzzy the Bunny," *Zap Comix* no. 5, 1970

*opposite,* "Fuzzy the Bunny" by Charles Crumb (excerpt), 1952

"Fuzzy the Bunny" by Charles Crumb

"Fuzzy the Bunny" by Charles Crumb

"Fuzzy the Bunny" by Charles Crumb

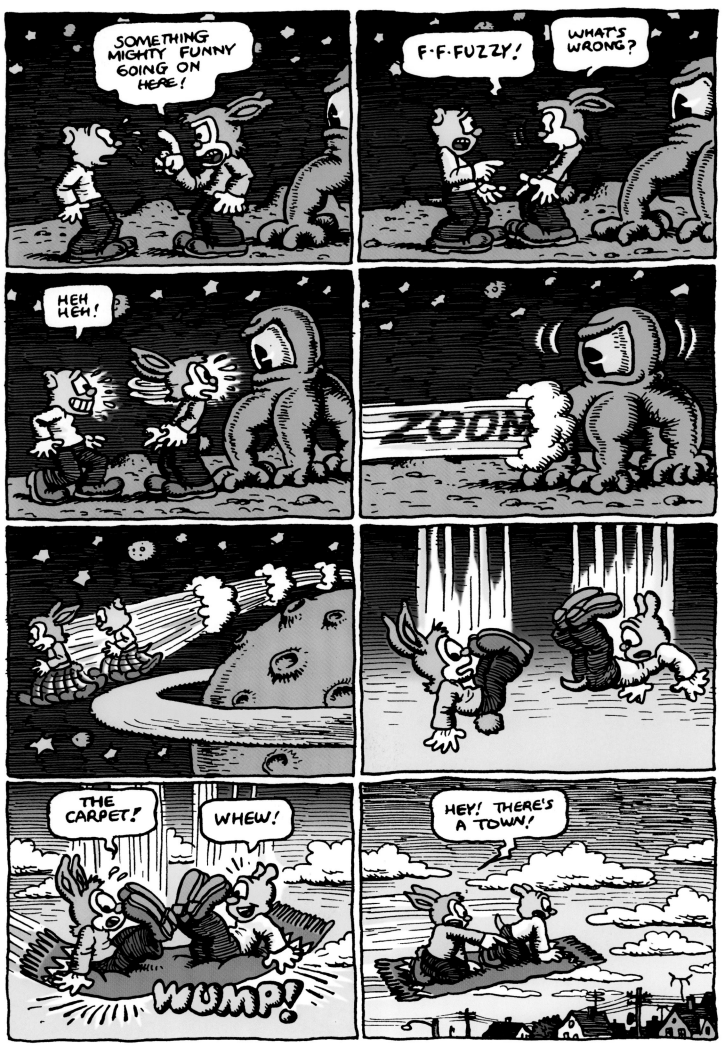

"Fuzzy the Bunny" by Charles Crumb

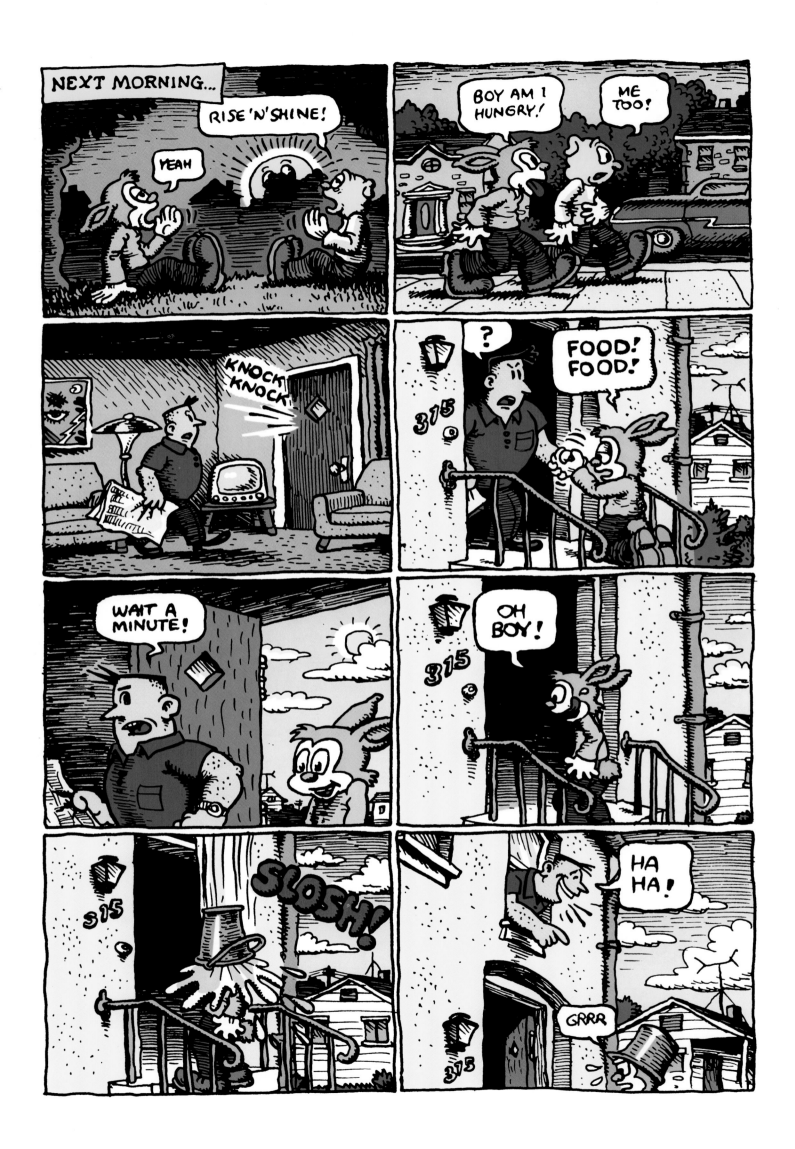

14

"Fuzzy the Bunny" by Charles Crumb

16

17

*above*, cover by Charles Crumb, early '50s; *opposite*, R. Crumb's version, late '60s

The Magic Kingdom: The Crumb kids visit Disneyland in 1956. *back*, Charles Crumb; *front row, left to right*, Sandra Crumb, Maxon Crumb and Robert Crumb

*"Treasure Island Days," Lemme Outta Here: Growing Up Inside the American Dream, 1978*

# "I CONSIDER THE BEST OF THE AMERICAN MEDIA OF THE OLD DAYS
## TO BE A CLASSICAL EDUCATION BY TODAY'S STANDARDS!"

I NEVER LIKED TO READ WAR COMICS, SUPER-HERO, CRIME, SCIENCE FICTION, HORROR OR WESTERN-TYPE COMICS WHEN I WAS A KID. THERE WAS TOO MUCH WRITING. IT WAS TOO MUCH WORK TO READ THEM. BESIDES, I WAS A SISSY, A MAMA'S BOY. I LIKED CUTE CHARACTERS. THOSE COMICS SEEMED SINFUL AND EVIL!

WE WERE VERY DISCRIMINATING. WHEN WE LOOKED AT MOST "FUNNY" COMICS ON THE RACK, LIKE *REAL SCREEN COMICS* OR *THE FOX AND THE CROW* — WE THOUGHT THEY WERE DUMB! COMICS FROM THE LATE FORTIES WERE GEMS TO US COMPARED TO WHAT WAS BEING PUBLISHED WHEN WE WERE COMING OF AGE AND LEARNING HOW TO DRAW OUR OWN COMICS IN THE FIFTIES. WHEN I FIRST SAW THE OCTOBER 1949 COVER OF *LITTLE LULU* (IN 1953 OR 1954), I WAS JUST DAZZLED BY IT! IT'S A BEAUTIFUL PIECE OF ARTWORK. THERE IS STILL SOMETHING MAGICAL ABOUT THESE COMICS TO ME. I REMEMBER WHEN THOSE *LITTLE LULU* COMICS WERE FIRST COMING OUT, WHEN I WAS 8, 9, 10 YEARS OLD. HOW FASCINATED I WAS BY THE STORIES, THIS CARTOON IMAGE OF THE WORLD I LIVED IN, THE MUNDANE WORLD OF LOWER-MIDDLE-CLASS AMERICA, PLAIN UNASSUMING HOUSES ON ORDINARY STREETS. IT WAS PRE-SUBURBAN AMERICA. SOME OF THE KIDS LIVED IN BRICK ROW HOUSES, OTHERS HAD LAWNS. THE MAIN THING, I GUESS, WAS THAT JOHN STANLEY WAS A GREAT STORYTELLER. HIS STORIES WERE SUBTLE, HUMOROUS AND PSYCHOLOGICAL. HE AND CARL BARKS WERE THE BEST STORY WRITERS IN THE "FUNNY" COMICS OF THE POSTWAR PERIOD. IT WAS ALWAYS A THRILL TO FIND AN OLD *LITTLE LULU* COMIC AT THE SALVATION ARMY STORE. FOR SOME REASON, THEY SEEMED HARDER TO FIND THAN OTHER DELL COMICS.

ONE DAY IN 1953, WE WERE WALKING HOME FROM SCHOOL — WE MADE IT A PRACTICE TO LOOK THROUGH TRASH CANS IN THE ALLEYS — WE FOUND A WHOLE BUNCH OF *LITTLE LULU* AND DISNEY COMICS, AND EVERY SINGLE ONE OF THEM HAD BEEN TORN IN HALF! WE TOOK THEM HOME AND TAPED THEM BACK TOGETHER. I HAD THOSE TAPED-UP ISSUES FOR YEARS, UNTIL I WAS IN MY TWENTIES, BECAUSE WE COULDN'T FIND OTHER COPIES.

IN NINTH GRADE, I DISCOVERED THE POLITICAL CARTOONS OF THOMAS NAST IN A BIG BOOK ABOUT THE HISTORY OF AMERICAN PRESIDENTS AT SCHOOL. I LOOKED AT THOSE NAST CARTOONS VERY, VERY CLOSELY! THERE WAS THE TAMMANY TIGER IN A ROMAN-STYLE ARENA MAULING MISS LIBERTY WHILE BOSS TWEED AS THE EMPEROR LOOKED ON. THE FEELING OF OLD-TIME AMERICA, THE WAY THE POST-CIVIL WAR ERA WAS CAPTURED AND THE WAY IT WAS DRAWN, INSPIRED ME TO LEARN TO CROSS-HATCH. I TRIED TO CROSS-HATCH WITH AN ORDINARY FOUNTAIN PEN. THIS WAS ALSO THE PERIOD WHEN I DEVELOPED AN INTEREST IN THE TWENTIES. LIVING IN THE LOWER MIDDLE CLASS, YOU WEREN'T EXPOSED TO ANYTHING OUTSIDE MAINSTREAM POP CULTURE, SO YOU FOUND THINGS IN RANDOM WAYS, IF YOU WERE CURIOUS, IF YOU WERE ON THE LOOKOUT.

I CAN REMEMBER BUYING COMICS IN THE EARLY FIFTIES AND SEEING MONTH AFTER MONTH THE QUALITY OF THE ARTWORK DECLINING. BY 1955-56, IT WAS OVER. IN 1953, I DISCOVERED *POGO POSSUM* BY WALT KELLY. I BECAME TOTALLY OBSESSED WITH HIM FOR A COUPLE OF YEARS! KELLY HAD A NOSTALGIA FOR OLD-TIME AMERICA. HIS CHARACTERS INHABITED A LITTLE WORLD THAT ATTRACTED ME. I DIDN'T COPY HIM DIRECTLY, BUT I IMITATED HIS DRAWING STYLE CLOSELY. I LIKED THE MEANDERING QUALITY OF HIS STORIES. THEY SEEMED PLOTLESS AND CASUALLY DONE. THE CHARACTERS TALKED TO EACH OTHER AND NOTHING MUCH HAPPENED. JUST A LOT OF FOOLISHNESS TAKES PLACE... WHICH I REALLY LIKED. KELLY'S DIALOGUE HAD A LOT OF PLAYS ON WORDS. IT WAS VERY LITERARY. WALT KELLY'S *POGO*, IN A WAY, PREPARED ME FOR HARVEY KURTZMAN'S *MAD*.

BY THE AGE OF 14, I HAD GONE THROUGH THE PAIN OF ADOLESCENT ALIENATION. I REALIZED I WAS A GEEK AND I WASN'T GOING TO MAKE IT WITH THE GIRLS. AT THIS POINT, MY PSYCHE WAS READY TO RECEIVE THE JOLT FROM *MAD* MAGAZINE!

INNOCENCE BETRAYED BY A PREDATORY ECONOMIC SYSTEM. CHILDREN ARE EASY PICKINGS...

BOB AT AGE 11, EATING HIS BREAKFAST ON SATURDAY MORNING STILL IN HIS PAJAMAS AND READING THE BACK OF THE WHEATIES BOX

*opposite*, inspirational penwork by Thomas Nast: the Tammany Tiger (detail), 1871; *above*, "Trash" (excerpt), *Weirdo* no. 6, 1982; *center*, sketchbook image, mid '80s

23

"Dumb," *Zap Comix* no. 13, 1994

I WASN'T THE **DUMBEST** BY ANY MEANS... IN COMPARISON TO MOST OF THEM I WAS ASSURED OF MY BRILLIANCE!

YOU GOT A NEAT CAR, WAYNE!

YOU BETTER B'LIEVE IT!

I'D CRACKED A FEW BOOKS, DROPPED OUT OF THE CHURCH, HAD A THIN GRASP OF SOCIALISM, WHICH MADE ME AN INTELLECTUAL **GIANT** AMONG MY PEERS!

OH THAT I'M FORCED TO DWELL IN CLOSE PROXIMITY TO SUCH MINDLESS YAHOOS!

SNORT!

CONSIDERING HOW DUMB MY PARENTS WERE IT'S NO WONDER I WAS SUCH AN IGNORANT BOOBISH PUDDING-HEAD!

WHO EVER HEARD OF A TEN-YEAR-OLD BOY WITH A TEDDY BEAR!?

YEAH YEAH DON'T GET YER BOWELS IN AN UPROAR, SARGE!

"EISEN-HOWER" JACKET

PEROX-IDE BLONDE

MY FATHER WAS A WORLD WAR TWO VETERAN. HE REVERED THE U.S. MARINE CORPS, IN WHICH HE SPENT TWENTY YEARS OF HIS LIFE. HE WALKED AROUND WHISTLING MILITARY ANTHEMS. "BRIDGE OVER THE RIVER KWAI" WAS A PARTICULAR FAVORITE.

GRRNNHH...

NO WONDER I ALMOST TURNED OUT A FAGGOT!

MY MOTHER WATCHED SOAP OPERAS ON T.V., AND UNDER THEIR MATTRESS YOU WOULD ALWAYS BE SURE TO FIND PLENTY OF LURID DETECTIVE MAGAZINES.

WOW, LOOKIT! THIS WOMAN GOT HER EYES AND TONGUE CUT OUT!!

PUT IT BACK! I HEAR HER COMING!

THEY WERE DECENT PEOPLE; DUTIFUL, HARD-WORKING, LAW-ABIDING... THEY MADE PERSONAL SACRIFICES SO THAT THE KIDS COULD HAVE NICE PRESENTS ON THEIR BIRTHDAYS AND CHRISTMAS...

OBOY! NEATO! JUST WHAT I WANTED!

GIMME IT!

THEY WANTED TO BE MODERN PEOPLE. AS SOON AS THE NEW "RANCH-STYLE" TRACT-HOMES WERE BUILT THEY BOUGHT ONE.

NICE "CAR PORT."..

I LOVE THE "PICTURE WINDOW"

AS SOON AS TELEVISION SETS BECAME AVAILABLE TO THE MASSES WE HAD ONE IN OUR HOUSE.

UNH... GRUNT

PANT

RIGHT OVER HERE, FELLAS..

JEEPERS!

OUR FAMILY SPENT MANY HOURS EVERY DAY SITTING IN FRONT OF THE "BOOB TUBE."... WE EACH HAD OUR PLACE...

I CAN STILL TO THIS DAY SING FOR YOU MANY COMMERCIAL JINGLES I LEARNED FROM TELEVISION FORTY YEARS AGO...

THERE'S SOMETHING ABOUT A MUNSE T.V. POPLAR - FIVE - OH - THREE - OH - THREE!

SEE THE U.S.A. IN YOUR CHEVROLET AMERICA IS ASKING YOU TO CALL...

USE AJAX THE FOAMING CLEANSER BUBUBUBU BUM BUM BUM —

MY BEER IS REINGOLD THE DRY BEER, THINK OF REINGOLD WHEN-EVER YOU BUY BEER, IT'S NOT SWEET, NOT BITTER, EXTRA-DRY FLAVORED TREAT —

HALO EVERYBODY HALO — HALO IS THE SHAMPOO THAT GLORIFIES YOUR HAIR —

PACKARD IS THE ONE FOR '51, ASK THE MAN WHO OWNS ONE.....

BETTER BUY BIRD'S EYE!

BRUSHA BRUSHA BRUSHA WITH THE NEW IPANA BRUSHA BRUSHA BRUSHA IT'S DANDY FOR YOUR TE-E-EETH!

PAMPER PAMPER NEW SHAMPOO, GENTLE AS A LAMB, SO RIGHT FOR YOU — GENTLE AS A LAMB. YE-E-ES MA'AM! PAMPER PAMPER NEW SHAMPOO!

BE SOCIABLE LOOK SMART STAY UP-TO-DATE WITH PEPSI! SO YOUNG AND FAIR AND DEBONAIRE —

TO LOOK SHARP, AND BE ON THE BALL, TO FEEL SHARP, DADA DA DADA TO BE SHARP, USE GILLETTE BLUE BLADES FOR THE SLICKEST QUICKEST SHAVE OF ALL!

REACH FOR A PEACH — A PEACH OF A BLEACH...

HEY MABEL BLACK LABEL

MAKES YA THINK, DON'T IT?

WE WENT TO CHURCH EVERY SUNDAY AND PERFORMED THE RITUALS ALONG WITH THE REST OF THE CROWD; KNEELING, STANDING, MAKING THE SIGN OF THE CROSS, ETC.

DOMINUS VOBISCUM ET COM SPIR-IMWU-----

OFTEN I WAS AFRAID I MIGHT PASS OUT DURING THE MASS.

THIS CHILDISH DEVOTION TO ROMAN CATHOLIC DOCTRINE AND PRACTICE GAVE ME A SMUG ATTITUDE OF MORAL SUPERIORITY OVER OTHER BOYS.*

C'MON CRUMB, STEP OVER THAT LINE! I DARE YUU! YA CHICKEN SHIT!

HAW HAW

THEY DON'T REALIZE HOW THEIR CONDUCT OFFENDS OUR LORD AND HIS MOTHER...

*BOYS WERE ONE THING—GIRLS WERE SOMETHING ELSE AGAIN...DISTANT, REMOVED, ANOTHER WORLD!

LATER, AFTER I'D ABANDONED THE CHURCH IN FAVOR OF INTELLECTUALISM, I HAD A NEW REASON TO FEEL SUPERIOR...

HEY, CRUMB, YOU BETTER STAY OUTA MY WAY, YOU FUCKIN' QUEER! I'LL STOMP YOUR FUCKIN' ASS!!

HE WILL, TOO, BWAH! YOU BETTER B'LIEVE IT!

IGNORAMUSES, INCAPABLE OF RISING ABOVE THEIR ANIMAL INSTINCTS!

IT WAS ALWAYS IMPORTANT TO ME TO THINK I WAS REAL SMART! "SMART" WAS ALL THE HIGH-SOUNDING IDEAS OUT OF THE LATEST BOOKS I'D READ.

I DUNNO, I'D LIKE TO THINK I COULD WORK IT OUT WITH BUZZY, BUT, Y'KNOW, HE'S GOT ALL THESE OTHER LITTLE CHICKIES HANGING AROUND, AND IT'S ONLY BECAUSE HE'S A MUSICIAN AND Y'KNOW, VERY CHARMING IN A BOYISH SORTA WAY...

I UNDERSTAND, LIZ, BUT...

DID YOU EVER STOP TO THINK THAT MAYBE THE ONLY REASON YOU LOVE BUZZY IS BECAUSE YOU ARE JUST A PRODUCT OF YOUR ENVIRONMENT, AND ALL YOUR THOUGHTS AND ACTIONS HAVE BEEN PREDESTINED BY THE PHYSICAL LAWS OF THE UNIVERSE?

SIGH... WELL, YES, YOU'RE RIGHT, ROBERT, THAT'S A BRILLIANT OBSERVATION, BUT, Y'KNOW, NOT REALLY HELPFUL TO MY SITUATION...

"WHAT IS MAN?" BY MARK TWAIN

NOT THAT YOU CAN'T LEARN THINGS FROM BOOKS; MORE PEOPLE SHOULD READ 'EM, BUT AS FOR THE REAL WORLD, MR. DEEP THINKER OVER HERE DIDN'T HAVE A CLUE, BECAUSE, WELL, I COULDN'T LOOK, COULDN'T FACE THEM HEAD ON... I WAS BLINDED BY A DEEP, POWERFUL REFLEX...

FEAR!

UH OH MOMMY MOMMY....

YES, I WAS AFRAID OF MY FELLOW HUMAN BEINGS...I WAS AFRAID OF THEIR JUDGMENT OF ME...

YEAH, SURE! ONE PERCENT OF THE TIME! AN INORDINATELY GREATER PART OF MY WAKING HOURS WERE SPENT JUST LIKE ALL THOSE OTHER CRASS YOUNG MALES I FELT SO SUPERIOR TO: FANTASIZING ABOUT **SEX!!**

HNH

HNH

HNH

THE POSSIBILITY THAT I WAS JUST LIKE ALL THE OTHERS IN THIS RESPECT DID NOT EVEN **DAWN** ON ME... NOR DID IT WORRY ME THAT I WAS UTILIZING MOST OF MY CREATIVE ENERGIES FOR MASTURBATION SCENARIOS...

PANT PANT

HNNH... LET'S EXPLORE THIS SITUATION...

I WILL SPARE YOU THE DETAILS. SUFFICE IT TO SAY THAT THESE FANTASIES HAD VERY LITTLE TO DO WITH REAL WOMEN OR "NORMAL" SEXUAL ACTIVITIES...

HAFTA GO LAY ON TH' BED NOW AN' THINK SOME MORE ABOUT THESE PICTURES I JUST DREW...

WOW!

WHOO-BOY!

THESE ARE **GOOD!!**

THEY WERE MY OWN ORIGINAL AND UNIQUE CREATIONS... BUT OF THIS I WAS NOT, AND NEVER HAVE BEEN, **PROUD.**\*

JOE MATT SYNDROME

Kleenex ®

PULL UP ONE UP POPS ANOTHER

\* LATER I EVEN HAD THE NERVE TO FOIST THESE ABSURD FANTASIES ON THE PUBLIC IN MY COMICS! WHY I THOUGHT ANYONE ELSE WOULD WANT TO SEE THIS STUFF I'VE FORGOTTEN.

QUITE THE CONTRARY... WHEN NOT USING THEM TO EXCITE MYSELF, AND ESPECIALLY IMMEDIATELY AFTER CUMMING, I EXPERIENCED STRONG FEELINGS OF **SHAME** AND **SELF-LOATHING**...

OHHH...

I GOTTA STOP DOING THIS...

IT WAS A VICIOUS CIRCLE.

LOOK AT THESE!

I'M SO **WEIRD!**

OH GOD I NEED **HELP!**

WHAT I NEEDED WAS A STINT IN THE ARMY. BOOT CAMP WOULD'VE DONE ME A WORLD OF GOOD....

BEING FORCED TO GO OUT INTO THE COLD, CRUEL WORLD AND GET A NINE-TO-FIVE JOB (ACTUALLY 8 TO 4:42) HAD ALMOST THE SAME EFFECT... I PICKED UP, AGAINST MY WILL, A BIT OF AUTHENTIC KNOWLEDGE AND EXPERIENCE OF LIFE... A TAD...

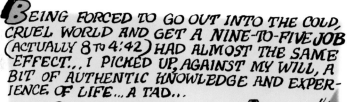

THEN I HAD A MAJOR SET-BACK... I DISCOVERED THE HIPPIES, QUIT MY JOB, AND STARTED GETTING "STONED."...

VERY QUICKLY I BECAME ANOTHER L.S.D. CASUALTY... YEP...

AND I HAD PLENTY OF COMPANY. "WE ALL LIVE IN A YELLOW SUBMARINE" WAS RIGHT! WE WERE VISIONARIES, HOLYMEN, FAIRY PRINCESSES, MYTHOLOGICAL GODS AND GODDESSES. IT WAS BEAUTIFUL...

TRYING VERY HARD TO LET MY BODY "FEEL" THE MUSIC (IT WAS HOPELESS)

MY SMUGNESS NOW REACHED TOWERING HEIGHTS, SURROUNDED AS I WAS BY OTHERS WHO SHARED THESE GRAND AND GLORIOUS ILLUSIONS... THEY WERE ALL MIDDLE-CLASS PUNKS LIKE ME...

IT TOOK ME TWENTY YEARS TO RECOVER FROM ALL THAT L.S.D. I TOOK... FOR A LONG TIME I WAS A MEDIÆVAL MAN LOST IN THE MODERN WORLD.

METAL PROJECTILES ON WHEELS... PEOPLE TRAPPED INSIDE... GOING TOO FAST... LIFE THREATENING... HARSH NOISES OF INFERNAL MACHINES... BY MY FAITH, AM I IN HELL??

BUT MAYBE L.S.D. WAS A GOOD THING IN SOME WAY... THE WAY IT CRACKED OPEN THE ARROGANT MINDSET OF TECHNO-INDUSTRIAL CIVILIZATION... MAYBE WE NEEDED THAT, I DUNNO... THE VERDICT'S NOT IN YET...

BUT, I —

KA-BOOM

STILL, I THINK I'M SOME SORT OF AN "IDIOT" BECAUSE OF L.S.D. *

NOW, IF WE TAKE A DEPRECIATION OVER THE NEXT FIVE YEARS AND AMORTISE THE INTEREST THAT SHOULD PUT YOU JUST UNDER THE 30 PERCENT BRACKET... YOU FOLLOW ME??

UHH... I GUESS SO...

* THAT'S RIGHT, BLAME IT ON DRUGS!

BUT AGAIN, I WASN'T THE DUMBEST HIPPY EITHER, AND AFTER A FEW BUMMERS I BEGAN TO GET DISILLUSIONED WITH THE HIPPIES...

MAN, THIS NEW SIDE BY THE "STONES" IS A FUNKY GET-DOWN STONE GROOVE!! GIVE IT ANOTHER SPIN, SUNSHINE... HERE, MAN...

UH YEH, SURE...

RIGHT ON!! THE STONES ARE SO FAR OUT! THEY'RE RILLY LIKE, A HIGH-ENERGY BAND!

OOPS

"HONKY TONK WOMAN" PLAYED TWENTY TIMES IN A ROW, I SWEAR TO GOD!

SKRAAAK

THEN I HAD ANOTHER SET-BACK... THESE L.S.D.-INSPIRED COMICS I'D DRAWN GAVE ME A MODEST KIND OF HERO STATUS IN THE SO-CALLED COUNTER-CULTURE...

HEY, R.! KEEP ON TRUCKIN', MAN!

YEAH HEH HEH

RAT ON, BRO'!

Y'KNOW, WHEN YOU'RE FAMOUS PEOPLE ARE EAGER TO BE YOUR FRIEND, SO THEY AGREE WITH EVERYTHING YOU SAY... YOUR OPINIONS AND IDEAS GO UNCHALLENGED...

I'VE BEEN THINKING—IT'S DIFFICULT TO PERCEIVE THE LARGER PATTERNS OF LIFE, THE — THE UPS AND DOWNS OF HUMAN SOCIETIES, CULTURES, CIVILIZATIONS OR WHAT-HAVE-YOU... TO TRY TO SEE YER-SELF, YOUR OWN PLACE IN THIS VAST SCHEME OF THINGS SO AS NOT TO BE Y'KNOW, A HELPLESS VICTIM OF HISTORICAL OR, AS IT WERE, SOCIAL CONFLICTS AND UPHEAVALS... INTERESTING, HUH??

HM!

GEE, YOU'RE SMART, ROBERT...

THANK YOU...

# "*I HAD SEEN THE FIRST ISSUE OF MAD* COMICS ON THE NEWSSTAND AND I REMEMBER BEING BEWILDERED BY IT! 'IT'S MELVIN!' WHAT DOES THIS MEAN?"

A SIGNIFICANT MOMENT FOR ME WAS THE FIRST TIME I SAW *MAD* #11 WITH THE *LIFE* MAGAZINE COVER. SEEING THIS RUDE, INSULTING LAMPOON OF THE GREAT *LIFE* WAS A REVELATION... BUT I COULDN'T READ THE STORIES... IT WAS TOO DENSE FOR ME, TOO MUCH TEXT! ANOTHER SUCH MOMENT WAS IN 1956 WHEN I FIRST SAW *MAD* #27, ONE OF THE EARLY 25¢ MAGAZINES, WITH A BEAUTIFULLY PAINTED COVER BY JACK DAVIS FILLED WITH HUNDREDS OF LITTLE FIGURES. IT'S AN UNBELIEVABLE COVER WITH EVERY SQUARE INCH COVERED WITH DETAIL! I COULDN'T BELIEVE MY EYES!

EARLY IN NINTH GRADE IN 1957, THIS GUY WILLARD STAYTON WAS WALKING AROUND WITH A *MAD* #29, SEPTEMBER 1956, WITH A WALLY WOOD COVER. IT WAS FUNKY, OFF-BEAT, BUT SO BEAUTIFUL, EVEN THOUGH THE COPY I HELD IN MY HANDS WAS BEAT TO HELL. I PESTERED WILLARD FOR DAYS TRYING TO GET IT OFF HIM! THEN I RAN DOWN AND BOUGHT THE MOST RECENT ISSUE ON THE NEWSSTANDS. BUT BY THEN, *MAD* HAD ALREADY PASSED ITS GREAT DAYS. BUT EVEN SO, THERE WAS *STILL* SOME GOOD WORK IN IT. AFTER FELDSTEIN TOOK OVER, *MAD* GRADUALLY BECAME MORE AND MORE CHILDISH AND ADOLESCENT... PROBABLY A DELIBERATE MARKETING STRATEGY. AS SOON AS I DISCOVERED IT AND STARTED BUYING IT, *MAD* BEGAN ITS LONG, LONG DOWNHILL SLIDE.

WE USED TO GO TO THIS TYPICAL TEENAGE SODA FOUNTAIN CALLED "THE CHATTERBOX," RUN BY AN OLD GUY THEY ACTUALLY CALLED "POP." SHORTLY AFTER I STARTED COLLECTING *MAD*, THERE ON THE MAGAZINE RACK OF THE CHATTERBOX, I FOUND *HUMBUG* NUMBERS 1 AND 2. *HUMBUG* WAS ANOTHER REVELATION FOR ME! THE "RADIATOR" COVER BY WILL ELDER WAS THE MOST BEAUTIFUL THING I HAD EVER SEEN UP TO THAT TIME! THE LOGO, THE RENDERING OF THE ARTWORK, THE FUNKINESS OF ITS ATTITUDE, AT THE SAME TIME HAVING THIS FEEL OF OLD-TIME AMERICA... I WAS FIXATED ON THIS STUFF AND STUDIED *HUMBUG* VERY CLOSELY. MY BROTHER CHARLES ALSO GOT INTERESTED IN THE KURTZMAN STUFF AT THIS TIME. JACK DAVIS, AL JAFFEE, ARNOLD ROTH ALL DID THEIR BEST WORK FOR *HUMBUG*. AND I USED TO LOOK AT THIS ARTWORK WITH AWE. JEEZIZ, IT'S BEAUTIFUL! WE WERE SO INSPIRED BY *MAD* AND *HUMBUG* THAT WE PUBLISHED OUR OWN SATIRE COMIC BOOK CALLED *FOO* IN 1958. IT LASTED THREE ISSUES.

*opposite*, Incredible cross-hatching by Jack Davis (detail), *Humbug* no. 8, 1958; *center*, Parody rules: cover by Basil Wolverton, *MAD* no. 11, 1954

I DIDN'T SEE *HUMBUG* FOR MONTHS AFTER FINDING THOSE FIRST TWO ISSUES AT THE CHATTERBOX. THEN MY PAL MIKE BRITT FOUND ISSUE 5! MY EYES POPPED OUT! I WROTE IN FOR A SUBSCRIPTION AND GOT BACK ISSUES 3 AND 4. ON THE LETTER PAGE IN *HUMBUG*, THERE WAS A LETTER FROM A GUY WHO PUBLISHED A FANZINE CALLED *SPOOF*, AND THAT OPENED UP A WHOLE WORLD TO CHARLES AND ME! DISCOVERING COMIC FANDOM BROKE US OUT OF THE ISOLATION OF OUR OWN LITTLE WORLD OF COMICS AND CHANGED OUR LIVES. WE FOUND OUT THAT YOU COULD ORDER OLD COMIC BOOKS FROM DEALERS. THAT WAS ANOTHER INCREDIBLE DISCOVERY! WE HAD SEARCHED HIGH AND LOW IN THE TOWN WE LIVED IN, AND HERE YOU COULD BUY THEM FOR FIFTY CENTS OR A DOLLAR FROM A DEALER. I REMEMBER WAITING FOR A PACKAGE OF OLD *MAD* COMICS TO ARRIVE, AND WHEN IT FINALLY DID, I COULDN'T BELIEVE IT! I WENT BACK AND STUDIED E.C. COMICS. I STOPPED DRAWING FUNNY ANIMALS ENTIRELY AND STARTED DRAWING *MAD* TYPE SATIRE STUFF. FELLOW FAN MARTY PAHLS STARTED CORRESPONDING WITH US AND THEN CAME AND VISITED US. WE GOT IN CONTACT WITH JOHN BENSON AND OTHER COMICS FANS.

THESE COMICS FANS LIVED IN A WORLD SURROUNDED BY PAPER. THEY WERE ALL VERY WORSHIPFUL ABOUT IT AND THAT BECAME A LITTLE TEDIOUS FOR MY BROTHER CHARLES AND ME BECAUSE WE USED COMICS AS AN INSPIRATION FOR OUR OWN WORK. MOST OF THEM WEREN'T CREATIVE GUYS ON THEIR OWN. THEY WERE JUST FANS. I FOUND IT A BIT DEPRESSING BECAUSE THEY SPENT ALL THEIR TIME CRITICIZING THIS STUFF AND NEVER DOING ANY CREATIVE WORK ON THEIR OWN. SO I JUST WANTED TO ABSORB THINGS AND THEN DO SOMETHING WITH THEM. IN THE END, IT WAS MY OWN WORK THAT WAS THE MOST INTERESTING TO ME.

IN MY EARLY TEENS, I'D BEEN TRAUMATIZED BY MY FAILED ATTEMPT TO PARTICIPATE IN THE VICIOUS WORLD OF TEENAGERS. I WAS JUST CRUSHED. I RETREATED TO MY ROOM. I STAYED HOME AND GOT MORE INTO MY ART. I FELT SO PAINFULLY ISOLATED THAT I VOWED I WOULD GET REVENGE ON THE WORLD BY BECOMING A FAMOUS CARTOONIST! I WAS VERY DETERMINED. THE AMAZING THING WAS THAT NOT LONG AFTER — A FEW YEARS, 1964 — I WAS WORKING WITH HARVEY KURTZMAN!

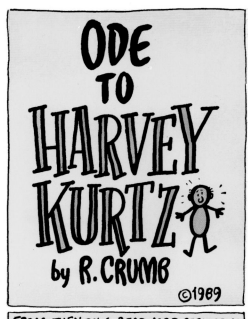

"Ode to Harvey Kurtzman," *Harvey Kurtzman's Strange Adventures*, 1989

*opposite*, Eyeball Kicks—cover by Jack Davis with border by Will Elder, *MAD* no. 27, April 1956

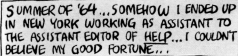

Cultural artifact:
cover by Will Elder,
with border by Jack
Davis, *Humbug*
no. 2, 1957

39

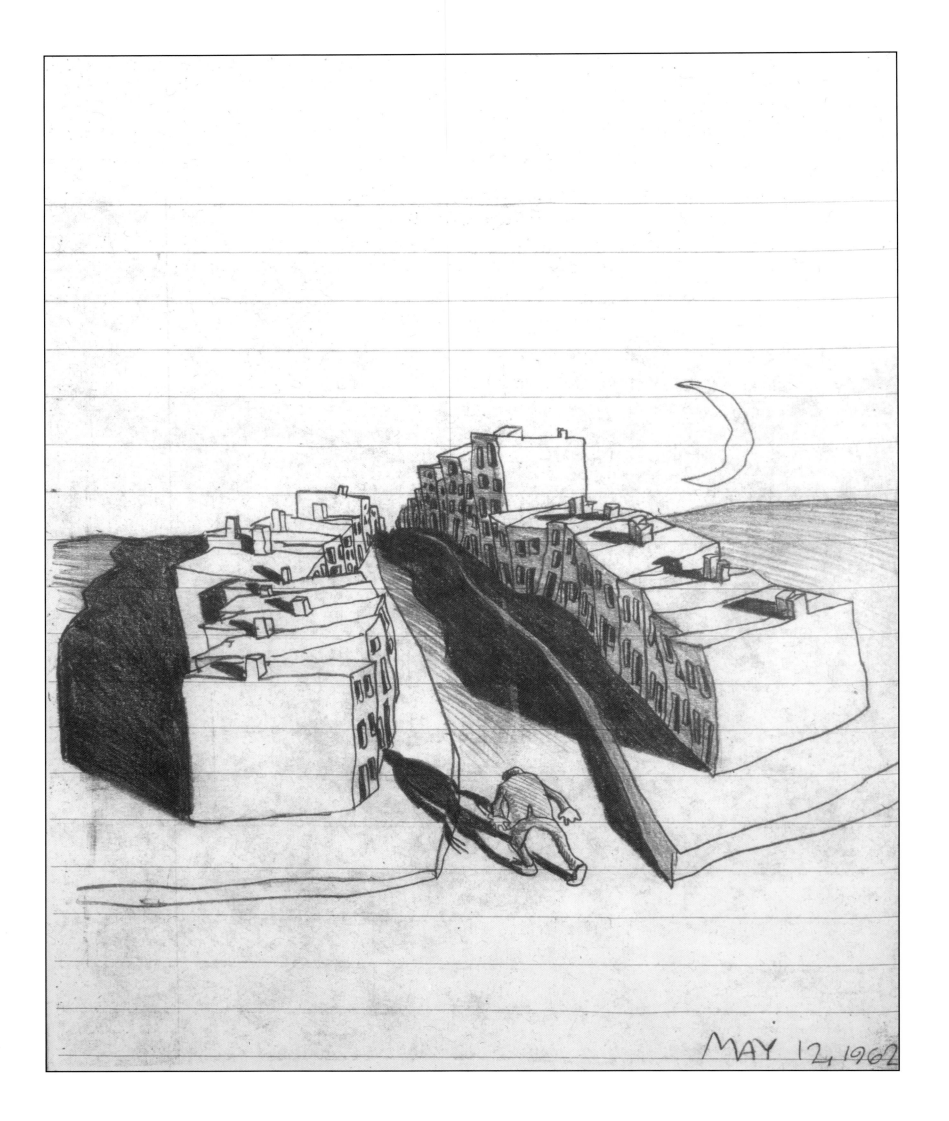

MAY 12, 1962

# "WHEN I LEFT HOME MY FATHER BOUGHT ME A BUS TICKET TO CLEVELAND AND LOANED ME $14."

OCTOBER 1962. I REMEMBER IT WELL. IT WAS A MOMENTOUS TIME IN MY LIFE. I HAD BEEN DEEPLY DEPRESSED AND DIDN'T KNOW WHAT I WAS GOING TO DO WITH MY LIFE. I HAD NO MONEY. I HAD MADE A LITTLE MONEY DOING AN OIL PAINTING OF SOME GUY'S HUNTING DOGS AND SPENT IT ALL BUYING OLD RECORDS. I HAD NO JOB. I HAD NO PLANS TO GO TO COLLEGE. I FELT VERY ISOLATED AND MOSTLY HUNG OUT WITH MY OLDER BROTHER CHARLES. MY PARENTS WERE FIGHTING ALL THE TIME. I WANTED TO GET OUT OF THERE REAL BAD. THEN MARTY PAHLS, WITH WHOM I HAD BEEN CORRESPONDING, GRADUATED FROM KENT STATE UNIVERSITY AND MOVED TO CLEVELAND. HE SUGGESTED I COME AND SHARE AN APARTMENT WITH HIM. I JUMPED AT HIS OFFER!

ALL I TOOK WAS A SUITCASE OF CLOTHES. MY PARENTS HAD BOUGHT ME A SUIT FOR MY HIGH SCHOOL GRADUATION AND IT WAS TAILORED TO FIT ME. I WENT AROUND APPLYING FOR STOCK CLERKING JOBS AT ALL THE BIG DEPARTMENT STORES IN CLEVELAND.

I WENT TO THE OHIO STATE EMPLOYMENT AGENCY AND FILLED OUT A FORM. THIS OLD GUY WHO WORKED THERE ASKED ME, WHAT COULD I DO? I SAID, "WELL, I'M AN ARTIST. I CAN DRAW PRETTY GOOD."

"OH, YEAH? YOU'RE AN ARTIST?"

"YEAH."

"YOU SURE YOU'RE GOOD?"

"I THINK SO. I HAVEN'T BEEN TO ART SCHOOL, BUT I DRAW PRETTY WELL."

HE SAYS, "OK, WE HAVE A GREETING CARD COMPANY HERE IN TOWN. I'LL GIVE THEM A CALL." I'M SITTING THERE IN THE OFFICE, AND HE CALLS THE PERSONNEL MANAGER OF AMERICAN GREETINGS AND TELLS HIM, "I GOT A KID SITTING HERE WHO'S AN INCREDIBLY TALENTED YOUNG ARTIST! YOU SHOULD SEE THIS KID'S WORK! IT'S REALLY AMAZING!" NOW, THE EMPLOYMENT GUY HADN'T SEEN ANYTHING I HAD DRAWN. THIS WAS ALL OFF THE TOP OF HIS HEAD. I KIND OF LAUGHED. I COULDN'T BELIEVE THIS. THE GUY HUNG UP THE PHONE AND LOOKED AT ME AND SAID, "WELL, NOW IT'S UP TO YOU! I DID WHAT I COULD. GOOD LUCK!"

I HAD AN APPOINTMENT FOR AN INTERVIEW AT AMERICAN GREETINGS BASED ON THE OLD GUY'S ENTHUSIASM. THE OLD GUY GOT ME THAT JOB. THE ART SAMPLES I HAD WITH ME INCLUDED SOME FAKE ALBUM COVER DESIGNS FOR REISSUES OF OLD-TIME MUSIC I MADE UP AND MY SKETCHBOOKS. THEY HIRED ME! IT WAS A MIRACLE—WITHIN TWO WEEKS OF ARRIVING IN CLEVELAND, I HAD A 40-HOUR-A-WEEK ART JOB! THE PAY WAS $60 A WEEK, AND I TOOK HOME $49. FROM MY FIRST WEEK'S PAY, I REPAID MY FATHER THE $14 HE HAD LOANED ME WHEN I LEFT HOME TO SEEK MY FORTUNE, AND I TOLD HIM THAT NEXT TIME, I'D SEND HIM THE BUS FARE. HE WROTE BACK AND SAID THAT WAS OK. I SHOULD KEEP THE BUS FARE AND START A SAVINGS ACCOUNT. IT WAS THE ONLY LETTER I EVER GOT FROM MY FATHER. A VERY SHORT PARAGRAPH... VERY TERSE. I WORE MY HIGH SCHOOL GRADUATION SUIT TO WORK EVERY DAY FOR TWO YEARS. I STILL HAVE THE NECKTIE.

WHEN I STARTED AT AMERICAN GREETINGS, THEY PUT ME IN A TRAINING PROGRAM WITH THE STIPULATION THAT I WOULD ATTEND ART SCHOOL. I SAID I WOULD BUT NEVER DID, AND THEY NEVER ASKED AGAIN. I STARTED OUT LEARNING TO USE AN AIRBRUSH AND CUTTING MASKS. YOU LEARNED TO MAKE A COLOR CHART USING EIGHT GREY TONES, FROM 10 PERCENT TO 80 PERCENT. IT WAS VERY HARD, VERY EXACTING, AND IF YOU DIDN'T HAVE IT FINISHED IN A MONTH, YOU WERE OUT OF THERE. THEN YOU HAD TO MAKE A WATERCOLOR RENDERING OF A ROSE IN GREY TONES ON ACETATE. THEY GAVE YOU A ROSE TO COPY AND YOU HAD TO DO IT HALF AN INCH BIG. THEY PUT OUT A LOT OF CARDS WITH FLOWERS ON THEM. AFTER FOUR MONTHS, THEY GRADUATED ME INTO COLOR SEPARATION. I GOT A FIVE-DOLLAR RAISE. I WAS THRILLED! THE COLOR SEPARATION DEPARTMENT WAS A HUGE FACTORY ROOM WITH LITTLE CUBICLES. THERE MUST HAVE BEEN 50 OR 60 DRAWING BOARDS IN THERE. AFTER A COUPLE OF MONTHS, I WAS THINKING ABOUT QUITTING. THE EXACTING WORK WAS TOO NERVE-RACKING! I WAS TOO SLOW. THEY WOULD GIVE ME FINISHED ART, SAY, A CUTE PUPPY DOG PAINTED IN A QUICKIE WATERCOLOR STYLE, VERY BLAND. I HAD TO DUPLICATE THIS THING FOR COLOR SEPARATION, WHICH WAS AN INCREDIBLY DAUNTING AND TEDIOUS PROCESS. OR A WATERCOLOR OF A FLOWER ARRANGEMENT. THIS OLDER ARTIST ROBERT LAISIG COULD PAINT ANY KIND OF FLOWER YOU WANTED ... FACILE, BREEZY, BUT THE COLOR SEPARATION— OH MY GOD! I ALWAYS TOOK TOO LONG, AND I STARTED TO DREAD GOING TO WORK.

MEANWHILE, I HAD GOTTEN TO KNOW THIS GUY LARRY RAYBOURNE, WHO WORKED THE HI-BROW DEPARTMENT. THE HI-BROW CARDS WERE THOSE TALL, HIP (FOR THE PERIOD) GREETING CARDS. HE BROUGHT HIS BOSS, TOM WILSON, DOWN TO SHOW HIM MY WORK (TO KEEP FROM GOING CRAZY I HAD COMPLETELY COVERED THE AREA AROUND THE GLASS OF MY LIGHT TABLE DRAWING BOARD WITH DOODLINGS— MILLIONS OF LITTLE DRAWINGS). TOM WILSON WAS VERY IMPRESSED WITH THAT, AND HE HIRED ME FOR THE HI-BROW DEPARTMENT. WHAT A LIFE-SAVER! IT WAS LIKE STEPPING UP FROM THE GALLEY TO THE CAPTAIN'S QUARTERS. IT WAS SUCH A CONTRAST. I GOT ANOTHER RAISE. FOR THE FIRST SIX MONTHS I DID ROUGHS FOR THE WRITERS OF THE LINES SO THEY COULD GET THEIR IDEAS APPROVED. THE BOSS, TOM WILSON, WHO LATER CREATED THE COMIC STRIP ZIGGY, PRAISED MY WORK BUT KEPT TELLING ME TO MAKE IT CUTER, LESS GROTESQUE. MY STUFF WAS "TOO GROTESQUE." SEE, 80 PERCENT OF GREETING CARD BUYERS ARE WOMEN, SO IT HAS GOT TO BE CUTE. THE HI-BROW STUDIO REALLY TAUGHT ME HOW TO DRAW CUTE. I FOUND IT HARD TO SHAKE THAT FORMULA. MAYBE AFTER 25 YEARS, I'VE SIFTED THAT CUTENESS OUT OF MY ART TO SOME EXTENT.

*opposite*, The Depths of Despair: sketchbook page, 1962; *right*, greeting card illustration, early '60s

*this page and opposite*, Cute Grotesques: greeting cards, early '60s

IT'S YOUR DAY, SO *RAISE HELL TONIGHT!*

# AMERICANS HAVE MADE SOME GREAT CONTRIBUTIONS TO THE WORLD!

Watt, who concocted the steam engine

Bell and his telephone

Edison, who had the bright idea of the lightbulb

Ford with his Model T

I DIDN'T THINK HE'D BE ABLE T' GET ANYTHING AS AN ARTIST BECAUSE TIMES WERE BAD AN' HE DIDN'T HAVE MUCH EXPERIENCE, BUT THEY LIKED WHAT HE SHOWED 'EM AT AMERICAN GREETINGS AN' HIRED HIM AS A COLOR SEPARATOR.

PAHLS AND CRUMB LIVED IN MY NEIGHBORHOOD AND WE GOT ALONG WELL SO I USED TO GO OVER TO SEE 'EM. MOSTLY WE'D TALK ABOUT JAZZ. AT THAT TIME I KNEW PAHLS ALOT BETTER THAN CRUMB. CRUMB WAS A PRETTY QUIET, RETIRING GUY.

WELL, ONE GUY I THINK YOU DEFINITELY OUGHTA LISTEN TO IS ~~~~

BUT I REMEMBER CRUMB AND I DID GO JUNK SHOPPING ONE TIME FOR OLD RECORDS. WE DIDN'T FIND ANY SIDES, BUT CRUMB DUG THE EXPERIENCE ANYWAY. WE WENT TO A PART A' TOWN HE WASN'T FAMILIAR WITH AND HE WAS REAL INTERESTED IN IT.

WELL WHADDYA KNOW—A WHITE SLUM...

CRUMB DID WIND UP LOOKING AT ONE A' THEM BIG OL' CONSOLE RADIOS WITH ALL THEM DIFFERENT BANDS AN' PUSH BUTTONS IN A USED FURNITURE STORE, THOUGH. HE REALLY LIKED OLD THINGS,...OLD MUSIC, OLD TOYS,... HE THOUGHT THEY HAD MORE CHARACTER THAN MODERN STUFF.

HEY, HOW MUCH Y' WANT FOR THIS?

"The Young Crumb Story" (excerpt),
*American Splendor* no. 4, 1979

ANYWAY, PAHLS AND CRUMB WERE REALLY INTA COMIC BOOKS. I KNEW SOMETHING ABOUT COMICS TOO, AND THEY GOT ME MORE INTERESTED THAN EVER...

YEAH, SEE THESE "PETER WHEAT" BOOKS ARE BY WALT KELLY... THEY'RE PRETTY RARE.

YEAH? C'N I SEE 'EM FOR A MINIT?

MEANWHILE, CRUMB WAS REALLY MOVING UP THE LADDER AT AMERICAN GREETINGS. HE GOT PROMOTED AND BECAME ONE OF THEIR TOP ARTISTS IN THE "HI-BROW" CARD DEPARTMENT.

PAT PAT

PEOPLE IN CLEVELAND STARTED TO GET HIP TO CRUMB'S ARTWORK AND REALLY LIKE IT. AS THEY DID HE STARTED TO COME OUT OF HIS SHELL SOCIALLY AND STARTED HANGING AROUND WITH A BOHEMIAN CROWD.

SSSSUCK

HE LIVED WITH PAHLS FOR A COUPLE OF YEARS BUT EVENTUALLY GOT HIMSELF A PLACE IN A HUGE APARTMENT WITH SEVERAL OTHER PEOPLE. I RE-MEMBER HIM TELLING ME HOW PLEASED HE WAS WITH ALL THE SPACE.

YEAH, THIS IS THE FIRST TIME I'VE ACTUALLY HAD MY OWN ROOM!

45

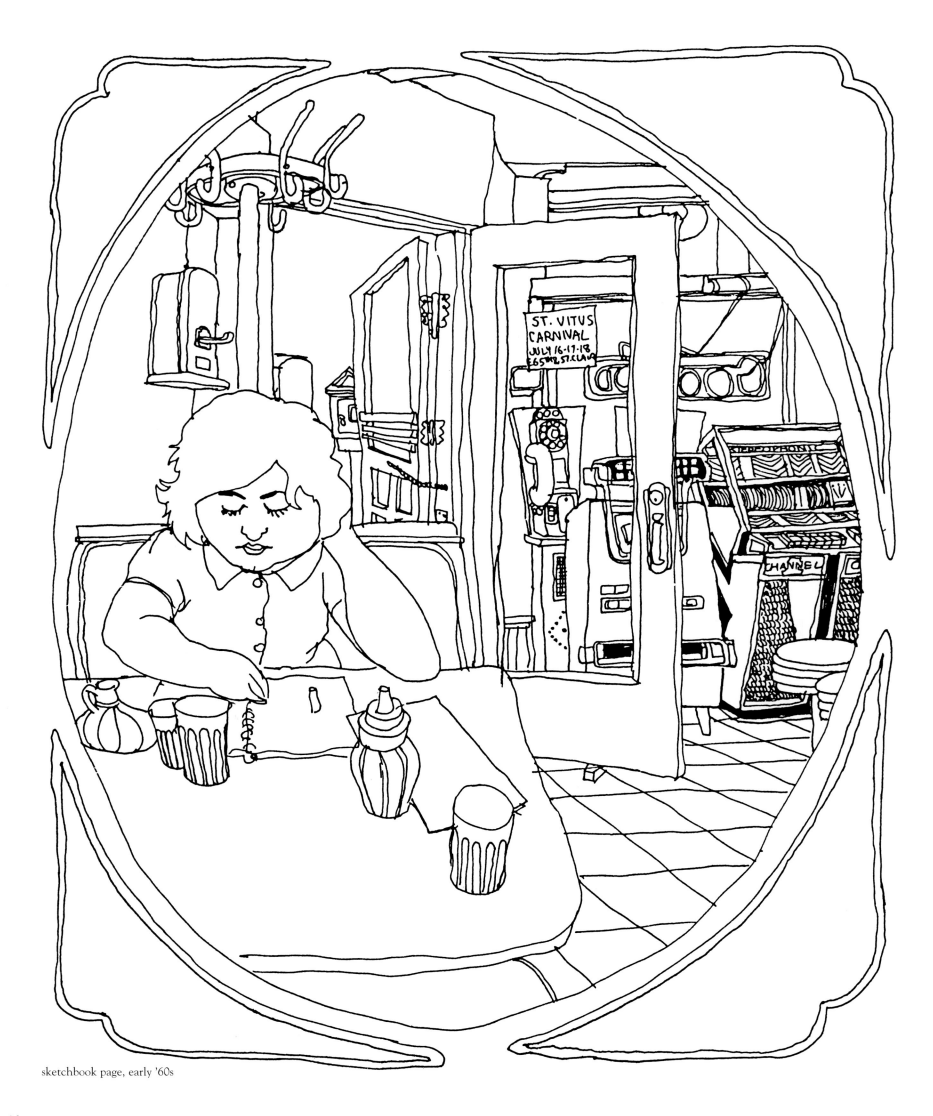

sketchbook page, early '60s

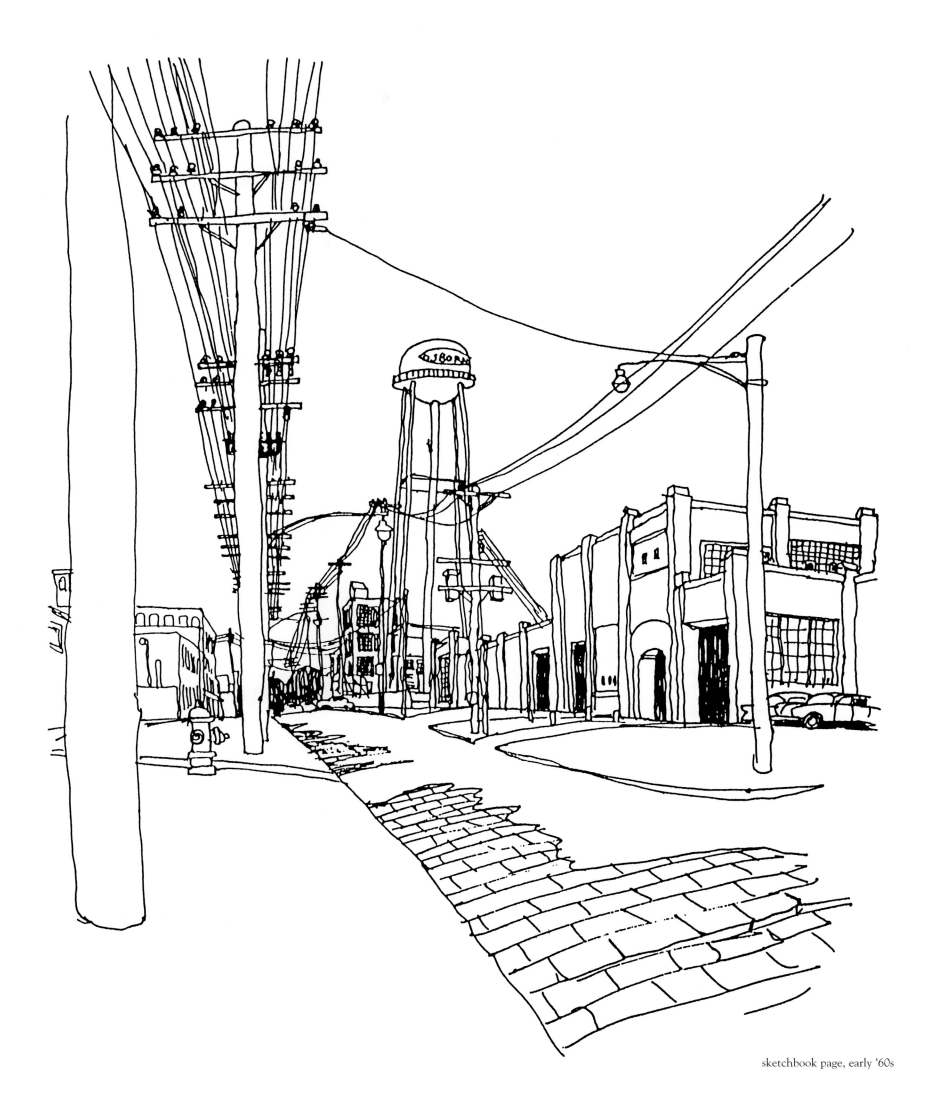

*sketchbook page, early '60s*

MY ASSOCIATION WITH HARVEY KURTZMAN BEGAN WHILE I WAS WORKING AT THE GREETING CARD COMPANY IN CLEVELAND. I HAD DRAWN THIS FRITZ THE CAT CARTOON, WHICH I SENT TO *HELP!* MAGAZINE'S "PUBLIC GALLERY DEPARTMENT." I GOT A NICE LITTLE LETTER BACK FROM KURTZMAN (WHICH I SAVED AND STILL HAVE) WHICH READ: "WE REALLY LIKED THE CAT CARTOON, BUT WE'RE NOT SURE HOW WE CAN PRINT IT AND STAY OUT OF JAIL." FRITZ THE CAT IS STRIPPING THIS GIRL CAT, AND IN THE LAST PANEL, HE'S PICKING FLEAS OFF OF HER. BUT THEY PRINTED IT THAT SUMMER.

KURTZMAN WAS VERY IMPRESSED BY MY SKETCHBOOKS. HE SENT ME OUT ON ASSIGNMENT TO HARLEM. I CAME BACK WITH SOME SKETCHES. KURTZMAN SAID, "YOU'VE GOT TO PUT IN SOME LITTLE FUNNY THINGS ABOUT IT. YOU CAN'T SIMPLY DO A DRAWING OR OBSERVATION. THIS IS A HUMOR MAGAZINE. IT HAS TO HAVE A PUNCH LINE OF SOME KIND. IT HAS TO HAVE A HUMOROUS ELEMENT." IN HARLEM, I WAS TOO NERVOUS TO STAND AROUND DRAWING ON THE SPOT. I WENT DOWN TO HARLEM THREE TIMES LOOKING AT THINGS CLOSELY, MAKING BRIEF SKETCHES AND WRITING DOWN THE NAMES OF BUSINESSES, BUT THEN THIS BLACK GUY CAME UP TO ME AND SAID, "GET OUT OF HARLEM, WHITE MAN!" AND I DID! I BEAT IT OUT OF THERE! I PUT THAT IN THE DRAWING. LATER WHEN I WAS DOING THE BULGARIA PIECE, I WAS THINKING MORE IN TERMS OF GAGS, BUT THAT'S HARD FOR ME. I CAN'T THINK THAT WAY, LIKE A COMEDIAN. KURTZMAN SAID, "DO IT FOR THE GUYS HANGING OUT ON THE CORNER." I TRIED.

LATER, AFTER *HELP!* FOLDED, KURTZMAN FELT RESPONSIBLE TO GET ME JOBS. HE SET ME UP WORKING WITH JACK DAVIS DOING SOME STORYBOARDS FOR TV COMMERCIALS, BUT DAVIS FIRED ME. HE SAID I WAS "TOO SLOW." KURTZMAN FELT GUILTY, SO HE GAVE ME THE OPPORTUNITY TO WORK WITH HIM AND WILL ELDER ON *LITTLE ANNIE FANNIE*. HE SAID, "WHY DON'T YOU TRY DOING SOME WATERCOLORS AND MAYBE WE CAN HAVE YOU HELP OUT ON THE BACKGROUNDS." SO I WENT HOME AND SPENT A WEEK OBSESSIVELY STRUGGLING WITH WATERCOLOR. I GOT OVER THE HUMP WITH THE MEDIUM, AND NOW I CAN WORK WITH IT PRETTY EASILY, BUT KURTZMAN LOOKED AT THE SAMPLES I DID AND SAID, "AHHH... YOU SHOULD KEEP DOING YOUR OWN STUFF. DON'T BE AN ASSISTANT TO ANYBODY! YOU'RE TOO ECCENTRIC AND INDIVIDUALISTIC!" KURTZMAN WAS ONE OF THE FEW OLDER PEOPLE IN MY YOUTH WHO GAVE ME GOOD ADVICE. HE GAVE ME SOME SOUND ADVICE ABOUT BUSINESS, WOMEN AND LIFE IN GENERAL.

After years of being a fan, Crumb did work for Harvey Kurtzman's *Help!* He contributed an early "Fritz the Cat" strip and sketchbook reports from Bulgaria and Harlem, where the photograph to the right was taken by Kurtzman's assistant editor, Terry Gilliam.

"Fritz Comes on
Strong," *Help!*
no. 22, 1965

50

52

unpublished
*Help!* page,
1965

53

"Harlem: A Sketchbook Report," *Help!* no. 22, 1964

THE
"DISCIPLES"
ARE FAR-OUT
WEIRDOS

THE
"UNTOUCHABLES"
... ONLY THEIR
HAIRDRESSER
KNOWS FOR
SURE...

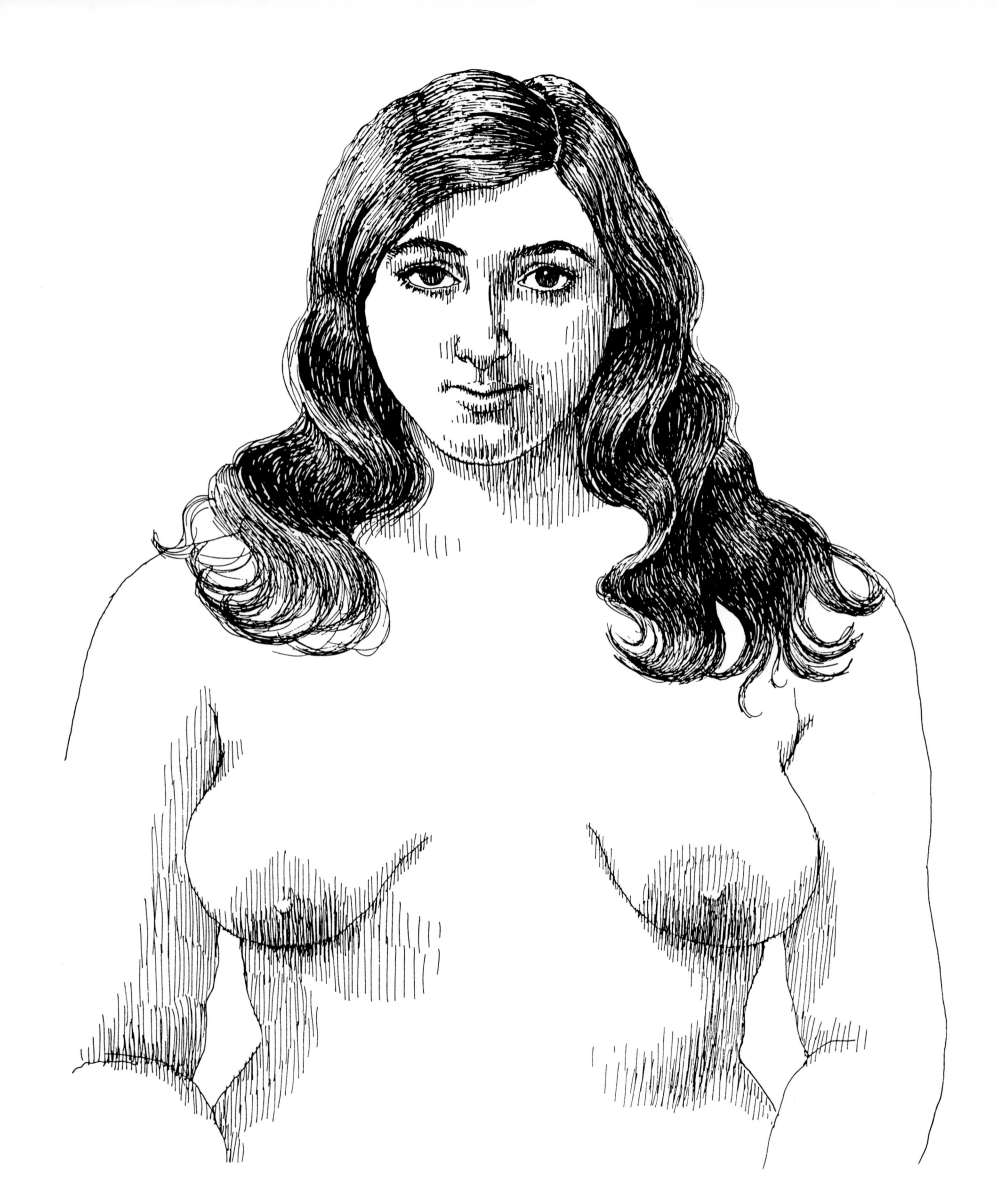

# "I WANTED TO BE ON MY OWN SO BAD...AND JUST WORRY ABOUT NO ONE BUT MYSELF..."

BUT IN SEPTEMBER 1964, I MARRIED MY FIRST WIFE, DANA. I WAS 21 YEARS OLD. BIG MISTAKE! I HAD QUIT AMERICAN GREETINGS AND GOT A SUMMER JOB IN ATLANTIC CITY WORKING IN A PORTRAIT GALLERY ON THE BOARDWALK. I GOT $2.50 FOR A PROFILE, $5 FOR A FULL-FRONT HEAD SHOT, AND SPLIT HALF OF EVERYTHING I MADE WITH THE GALLERY. DANA TRACKED ME DOWN IN ATLANTIC CITY THROUGH MY FAMILY. WE GOT MARRIED AND WENT TO EUROPE ON OUR HONEYMOON. WE HAD THAT *EUROPE ON $5 A DAY* BOOK. WE WENT TO LONDON AND THEN ON TO SWITZERLAND. IN ZURICH, DANA TOTALLY FREAKED OUT BECAUSE EVERYONE WAS SPEAKING A FOREIGN LANGUAGE. WE ENDED UP IN LOCARNO, IN SOUTHERN SWITZERLAND, RENTING ROOMS FROM A LONELY OLD LADY WHO WOULD COME AND SIT IN OUR KITCHEN AND TELL US WAR STORIES. I DID A LOT OF SKETCHBOOK STUFF. I DREW "FRITZ BUGS OUT" THERE. I TOOK CARD ROUGHS FROM AMERICAN GREETINGS AND WOULD SEND THE FINISHED ART BACK AND GET A CHECK IN THE MAIL.

HARVEY KURTZMAN SENT ME $300 TO GO TO BULGARIA TO DO AN ILLUSTRATED FEATURE FOR *HELP!* DANA AND I TOOK THE *ORIENT EXPRESS* AND GOT OFF IN SOFIA IN THE MIDDLE OF THE NIGHT. WE SPENT A WEEK IN THE BULGARIA, TOOK PHOTOS AND I DREW IN MY SKETCHBOOK. KURTZMAN ONLY USED PART OF WHAT I SENT HIM. WE MOVED TO COPENHAGEN, WHERE THE AMERICAN GREETINGS CARD CHECK WAS ALWAYS LATE IN COMING. WE HAD NO MONEY. NOT A CENT! DANA WENT OUT AND STOLE FOOD. I DREW SOME STRIPS CALLED "THE SILLY PIGEONS" AND "FRITZ THE CAT, SPECIAL AGENT FOR THE C.I.A." BECAUSE I HAD A COUPLE OF JAMES BOND NOVELS AND THOUGHT THEY WERE RIDICULOUS. WE DIDN'T KNOW WHAT WE WERE DOING. WE WERE JUST A COUPLE OF IDIOTS. WE RETURNED TO CLEVELAND FROM EUROPE AND I ENDED UP BACK AT AMERICAN GREETINGS ... APRIL OF 1965.

AT FIRST, BEING MARRIED WAS NICE, BUT AFTER SIX MONTHS, I BEGAN TO FEEL VERY RESTLESS, VERY TRAPPED. I WANTED TO ESCAPE BUT THEN I WAS ALSO TORN BY GUILT. IT WAS AWFUL. IN 1967, IN SAN FRANCISCO IN THE MIDDLE OF THE "SUMMER OF LOVE," I SAID, "I CAN'T TAKE ONE MORE MINUTE OF THIS!" WHILE DANA WAS OUT SHOPPING, I WENT OUT ON THE STREET AND STARTED HITCHHIKING. I DIDN'T HAVE ANY MONEY. I HAD MADE A SIGN SAYING "CHICAGO," BUT I WASN'T AWARE THAT I HAD SPELLED IT WRONG. IT SAID "CHIGAGO." IT WASN'T UNTIL TWO DAYS LATER THAT SOMEBODY POINTED IT OUT TO ME.

HITCHHIKING CROSS-COUNTRY WAS A LOT HARDER THAN I THOUGHT. IN SOME STATES PEOPLE WILL NOT PICK YOU UP. I GOT A RIDE IN A SEMI, ONE OF THOSE GREAT BIG TRACTOR TRAILER RIGS AND GOT LET OFF IN FERNLEY, NEVADA, WHERE I SPENT EIGHT HOURS IN THE DESERT. THERE WAS A LIGHT POLE THERE ON WHICH PEOPLE WHO HAD BEEN STRANDED THERE WROTE CURSES. ONE GUY HAD BEEN STRANDED THERE TWENTY-ONE HOURS. THERE WERE BITS OF STALE BREAD AND ORANGE PEELS AROUND ON THE GROUND. I FINALLY RAN JUMPING UP AND DOWN SCREAMING AFTER THIS HIPPY VAN WITH A BIG PEACE SIGN PAINTED ON IT TO GET A RIDE OUT OF THERE. THIS DOOFUS HIPPY GUY WHO WAS STONED WAS DRIVING. ALL HE COULD SAY WAS, "YEAH, THAT'S COOL, TOO!" THE VAN WAS LIKE AN OLD MILK TRUCK AND THE INSIDE BACK WAS DRAPED UP INSIDE LIKE SOME HIPPIE PAD. HE HAD ALSO PICKED UP TWO RUNAWAY GIRLS AND A VERY REFINED CUTE BOY FROM BOSTON. THE NEXT MORNING THE COPS STOPPED US AND TOOK THE DRIVER AND THE GIRLS AWAY. THE COPS SAID THEY'D ARREST US IF THEY CAUGHT US HITCHHIKING OUT OF TOWN. THE GUY FROM BOSTON AND I WANDERED AROUND ALL DAY. WE ENDED UP RIDING THE RAILS. IT WAS A CRAZY THING TO DO. BUT AT THE TIME I DIDN'T SEE IT AS A ROMANTIC THING BUT AS A NECESSITY. WE WERE OBLIVIOUS TO THE DANGERS. I'M SURPRISED I COULD EVEN FIGURE OUT WHERE THESE TRAINS WERE GOING. WE JUST JUMPED ON A FLAT CAR AND THE NEXT DAY WE WERE IN CHEYENNE, WYOMING. WE TRIED TO HITCH HIKE OUT OF CHEYENNE AND WALKED FIVE MILES OUT TO THE EDGE OF TOWN. THERE WERE TEN HIPPIES THERE AND NOBODY WAS STOPPING. BY EVENING WE WERE AT THIS RESTAURANT STARING AT THE PIE RACK WITH FIFTY CENTS BETWEEN US... "OH MAN WHAT KIND OF PIE SHOULD WE GET?" THIS YOUNG WAITRESS SAW US AND SAID, "SIT DOWN. I'LL GIVE YOU A COUPLE OF HAMBURGERS." WE LOOKED AT HER IN TOTAL AMAZEMENT! OUR FAITH IN HUMANITY WAS RENEWED AS WE GOBBLED DOWN THOSE BURGERS! THAT SINCERE REFINED GUY FROM BOSTON WAS A LUCKY CHARM FOR ME. HE WAS LIKE HENRY FONDA AND I WAS LIKE JOHN CARRADINE IN *THE GRAPES OF WRATH*. WE CAUGHT ANOTHER TRAIN AND RODE IN CULVERT PIPES THAT WERE TIED TO A FLAT CAR TO NORTH PLATTE, NEBRASKA, WHERE A RAILROAD DETECTIVE GAVE US TWO CHOICES: "YOU BOYS CAN EITHER GO TO JAIL FOR THIRTY DAYS OR YOU CAN PAY AND TAKE A PASSENGER TRAIN OUT OF HERE!" HE WAS A GRUFF KIND OF CHARACTER, BUT NOT MEAN. HE WAS LOOKING THROUGH MY SKETCHBOOK AND STARTED LAUGHING AT THE DRAWINGS. I WIRED DANA FOR $100 AND WE TOOK THE PASSENGER TRAIN TO CHICAGO. IT WAS VERY STRANGE TO BE ACTUALLY SITTING IN A SEAT OF A PASSENGER TRAIN WHEN A SHORT TIME BEFORE I HAD BEEN RIDING IN A CULVERT PIPE.

*opposite*, sketchbook drawing of Dana Crumb, 1964-65; *center*, Crumb in Bulgaria, 1964; *above*, "The Silly Pidgeons" excerpt, 1965

sketchbook page,
1965

sketchbook page, 1965

# The Silly Pidgeons

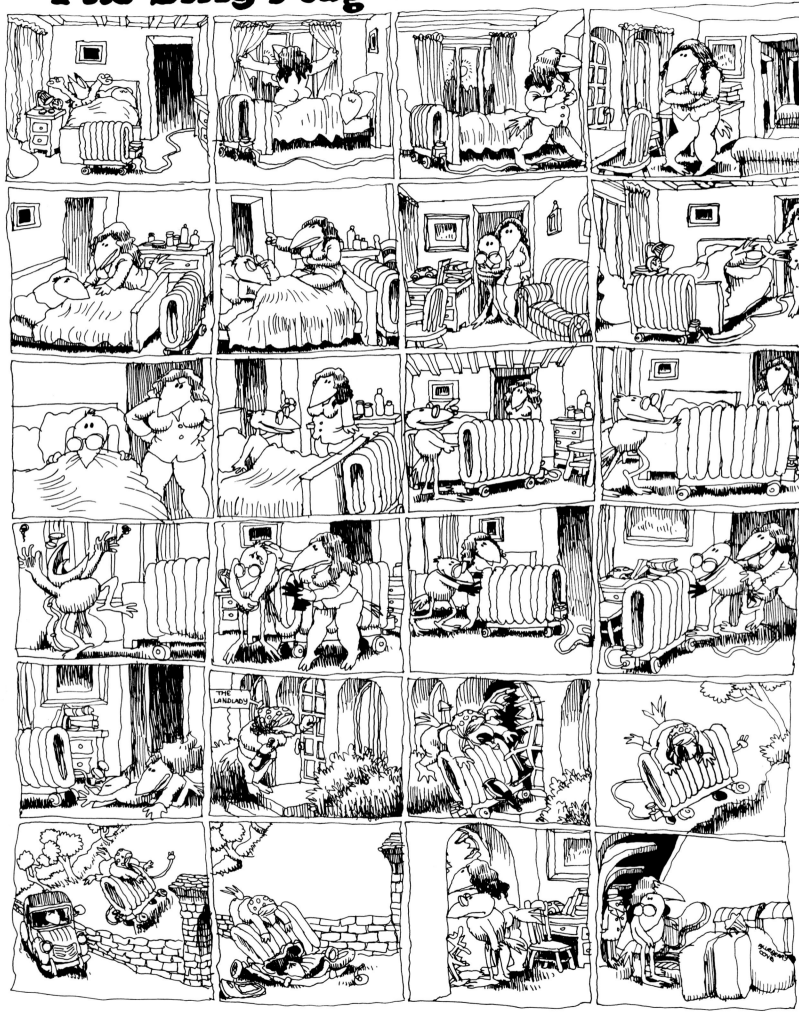

ARRIVED IN SOFIA IN THE MIDDLE OF THE NIGHT... GETTING A TAXI WAS A REAL BITCH....

SINCE THE REVOLUTION, BULGARIA'S CAPITAL HAS MUSHROOMED INTO A MODERN METROPOLIS.

*opposite,* "The Silly Pidgeons," 1965; *this page,* "Bulgaria: A Sketchbook Report" (portion not published in *Help!*), 1965

I WAS TOLD TO GO TO THE COMMITTEE
FOR FRIENDLY FOREIGN RELATIONS....

AT THE OFFICIAL TOURIST AGENCY....

AND THEN THERE WAS THIS YOUNG FELLOW WHO WORKED
AS AN ELECTRICIAN WHOM I MET IN A COFFEE SHOP....

# THERE WAS AN ART STUDENT AT THE NATIONAL ACADEMY....

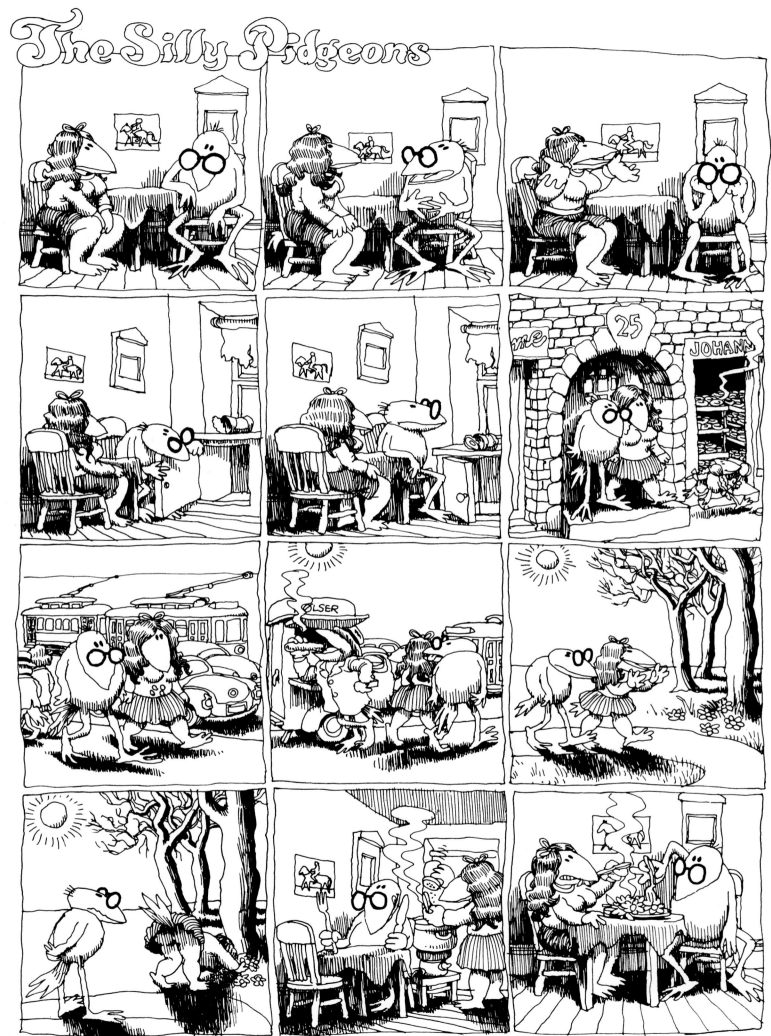

"The Silly
Pidgeons," 1965.
This autobio-
graphical strip
was drawn during
hungry days in
Denmark.

"The Silly Pigeons," intended for *Help!*, 1965

# "LSD WAS LEGAL IN 1965, THE FIRST TIME I TOOK IT!"

DANA GOT OUR FIRST LSD FROM A PSYCHIATRIST. IT WAS A BLUISH LIQUID IN LITTLE GLASS VIALS, MADE AT SANDOZ PHARMACEUTICAL COMPANY IN SWITZERLAND. THE BEST. THE FIRST TRIP WAS A COMPLETELY MYSTICAL EXPERIENCE; SHOCKING, FRIGHTENING AND VISIONARY. I WANTED TO DO IT AGAIN. DANA HEARD THAT SOME PEOPLE WERE HANDING OUT LSD, SO ONE NIGHT WE WENT TO THIS BIG FANCY OLD HOUSE IN CLEVELAND HEIGHTS. THERE WAS NO FURNITURE, BUT I AUTOMATICALLY ASSUMED THAT THEY HAD A LOT OF MONEY. THEY SEEMED LIKED RICH KIDS. IT WAS A STRANGE SCENE. I TOLD THEM I WANTED A VERY POWERFUL DOSE. WHAT THEY GAVE DANA AND ME WAS GOOD STUFF, VERY PURE, BUT I BECAME VERY FRIGHTENED OF THESE PEOPLE ONCE THE DRUG TOOK HOLD. THEY BECAME DEMONS TO ME... DEVILS. I THOUGHT I WAS IN *HELL!* I BELIEVED IT! AT A CERTAIN POINT, I REMEMBER COMING OUT OF THESE DEPTHS OF HORROR AND FORCING MYSELF TO FORGET SOMETHING I HAD SEEN BECAUSE IT WAS TOO HORRIBLE AND I COULDN'T HANDLE IT! THE ONLY WAY I COULD COME BACK FROM THIS TRIP WAS TO FORGET WHAT I WAS SEEING, AND I THREW UP ON THE FLOOR!

THOSE PEOPLE WERE TOTALLY DISGUSTED WITH ME. I DIDN'T KNOW WHO THEY WERE OR WHETHER THEY WERE GOVERNMENT AGENTS OR JUST SOME OBNOXIOUS FRATERNITY BOYS WITH THEIR GIRLFRIENDS ON A LARK.

A COUPLE OF WEEKS LATER, I WANTED TO GET A LOOK AT THESE PEOPLE SOBER AND SEE WHAT THEY WERE ABOUT. I CALLED UP AND THEY INVITED US BACK. WE SAT AROUND SMOKING MARIJUANA AND WATCHING A CRYSTAL LIGHT SHOW THAT THIS SCIENTIST GUY HAD CREATED. HE HAD CREATED A WAY TO PROJECT THESE CRYSTAL FORMS ON A SCREEN AND THE HEAT IN THE PROJECTOR WOULD MAKE THE CRYSTAL SHIFT. IT WAS BIZARRE. THERE WAS THIS OTHER YOUNG GUY THERE WHO THEY HAD GIVEN LSD TO, AND HE WAS TAKEN INTO ANOTHER ROOM BY THIS ALPHA-MALE-TYPE GUY JUST AS THEY HAD DONE WITH ME. WHEN I HAD TAKEN THEIR LSD, THIS GUY HAD TRIED TO BE MY GUIDE OR SOME BULLSHIT LIKE THAT. I DON'T KNOW IF THE GUY WAS JUST INEPT AT IT OR WHAT, BUT HE JUST TERRIFIED THE HELL OUT OF ME! SO HE TAKES THIS KID INTO THE OTHER ROOM TO BE HIS GUIDE ON LSD, AND SUDDENLY WE HEAR THIS BLOOD-CURDLING SCREAM! WE ALL RUSHED IN THERE, AND THIS KID WAS CRINGING IN THE FETAL POSITION ON A MATTRESS ON THE FLOOR. THE SCHMUCKY ASSHOLE "GUIDE" WHO WAS SITTING OVER HIM TRYING TO SOOTHE THIS KID TURNED TO US AND SAID, "YOU ALL HAVE TO LEAVE NOW! THIS IS A HEAVY SITUATION I HAVE TO DEAL WITH! YOU'D BETTER GO!" SO WE LEFT. I REALLY DIDN'T KNOW WHAT TO THINK...WERE THEY EXPERIMENTING ON PEOPLE WITH LSD? THE GUY WAS NOT A "HIPPIE" TYPE. HE WAS A VERY UPPER-CLASS RULING-ELITE TYPE. IT WAS WEIRD, VERY WEIRD.

LATER, WHEN DANA AND I LIVED IN SAN FRANCISCO, THE SCIENTIST GUY AND HIS GIRLFRIEND VISITED. THEY WERE STRANGE. ON THAT LSD TRIP IN CLEVELAND, THE GIRL (ALTHOUGH VERY ATTRACTIVE) HAD LOOKED LIKE A FEMALE DEMON TO ME! I HAD DRAWN HER WITH DEMONIC EYEBROWS IN MY SKETCHBOOK DRAWING THAT SAYS, "THIS IS HELL." SHE WAS SEXY AND EVERYTHING, BUT THERE WAS SOMETHING ABOUT HER THAT WAS HARSH AND SCARY. THEY WANTED TO GO TO THE AVALON BALLROOM. SHE SAID, "I WANT TO MAKE MYSELF UP TO LOOK REAL BIZARRE AND STRANGE WHEN WE GO TO THIS PLACE! WHY DON'T YOU HELP ME?" SO I STRADDLED HER WHILE SHE SAT IN A CHAIR AND PAINTED HER FACE TO LOOK LIKE THE DEMON I HAD SEEN HER AS ON LSD! SHE GOT A BIG LAUGH OUT OF IT WHEN SHE LOOKED IN THE MIRROR.

LSD WAS NEVER EASY FOR ME. I ALWAYS HAD HORRIBLE NIGHTMARISH EXPERIENCES AND COSMIC WONDROUS EXPERIENCES LIKE THE UPS AND DOWNS OF A ROLLER-COASTER RIDE. I COULDN'T UNDERSTAND PEOPLE WHO WOULD DROP ACID TO HAVE A GOOD TIME OR HAVE SEX. IT WAS UNTHINKABLE! I WOULD BECOME A QUIVERING MASS, TWISTING AND TURNING ON A SWEAT-DRENCHED MATTRESS, NOT ABLE TO FUNCTION AT ALL.

I REMEMBER TAKING ACID WITH MY FRIEND JOEL DEUTSCH. THIS WAS IN SAN FRANCISCO, AND WE TOOK THE BUS ALL THE WAY OUT TO THE BEACH... THE END OF THE LINE. WE WALKED AROUND "PLAYLAND" FOR A WHILE AND THEN WALKED OUT TO THE OCEAN AND SAT DOWN ON THE SAND LOOKING OUT AT THE WATER. I BECAME PART OF THIS TIMELESS CYCLE OF WAVES, THIS ETERNITY OF WAVES HITTING THIS BEACH FOR MILLIONS OF YEARS. SITTING THERE I FELT COMPLETELY OUTSIDE OF TIME. SUDDENLY JOEL SAYS, "I THINK WE SHOULD GO NOW." HUH? GO? WHAT? I HAD TO LEAVE ETERNITY AND COME BACK INTO TIME. WE TURNED AROUND TO GO, AND I SAW THE CITY! I HAD FORGOTTEN IT! THERE IT WAS, CIVILIZATION! AND IT STRUCK ME AS SUCH AN ILLUSION, SUCH FOLLY, SUCH AN ABSURD CONSTRUCT: THESE BUILDINGS, STREETS, CARS, SIGNS...THIS IS CRAZY!

THAT'S HOW THE HIPPIES GOT TUNED INTO THE CYCLES OF NATURE, WHICH EXIST OUTSIDE MAN'S CONSTRUCTS. WE COME FROM ALL THAT — PART OF US IS STILL MOST COMFORTABLE WITH MOTHER NATURE. OUR CIVILIZATION IS SOMETHING WE CREATE, BUT IT IS ALSO ALIEN TO US IN SOME WAYS.

JUST LIKE BEIN' BORN STONED

*opposite and above*, Two versions of a cover for a never-published comic book, 1967 and 1966 respectively. The title was later used for R. Crumb's *Head Comix*, a book collection from 1968. *right*, "Stoned" excerpt, *Cavalier*, October 1967

"My First LSD Trip," *El Perfecto Comics*, 1973

*opposite*, sketchbook drawing, 1965

69

This sketchbook page from 1965 demonstrates the transition from naturalistic drawing to drawing influenced by LSD.

*opposite*, sketchbook page, 1966-67

This sketchbook page (1965-66) contains the first Mr. Natural strip.

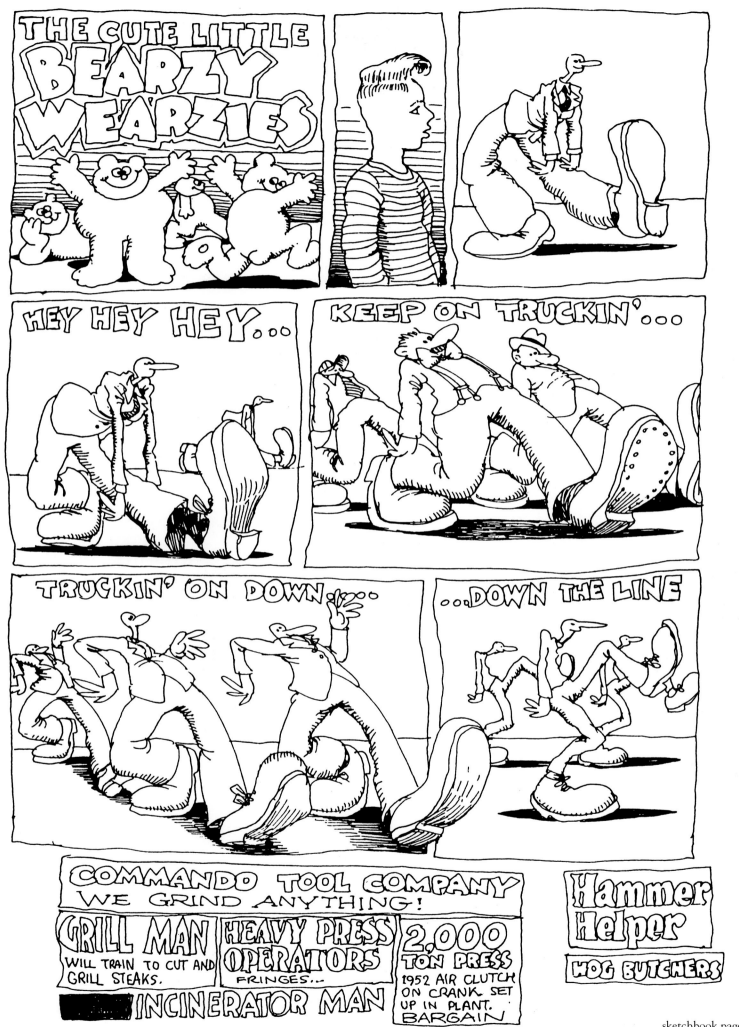

sketchbook page, 1966-67

# "STARTING IN THE MID-SIXTIES I WOULD SPIN OUT ALL KINDS OF IDEAS FOR CARTOONS IN SKETCHBOOKS!"

IT STARTED AS A KID WHEN WE WOULD MAKE OUR OWN HOME-MADE COMICS. WE DEVELOPED THE HABIT OF FILLING UP NOTEBOOKS WITH STUFF. I JUST CONTINUED WITH THAT AND GOT INTENSELY INTO DRAWING (NOT JUST COMICS) IN MY LATE TEENS. I STARTED LOOKING AT THE OLD MASTERS IN BOOKS ... LEONARDO, EVERYBODY. I THOUGHT I WANTED TO DRAW LIKE THAT, SO I DREW LIKE A MOTHERFUCKER! THAT WAS A BREAKTHROUGH. I DIDN'T USE PENS AND INK UNTIL I WAS 20. AT AMERICAN GREETINGS, WE USED RAPIDOGRAPH PENS TO DO THE INKING ON THOSE STUPID GREETING CARDS. I GOT TO KNOW THIS YOUNG WOMAN ARTIST NAMED LIZ JOHNSTON. SHE ENCOURAGED ME TO USE THE RAPIDOGRAPH TO GO OUT AND DRAW FROM LIFE. SHE TOOK ME OUT WITH HER. I STARTED DOING CONTOUR DRAWINGS FROM LIFE WITHOUT ANY PENCILING AT ALL. IT WAS REALLY GOOD PRACTICE AND TAUGHT ME A LOT, BECAUSE YOU HAVE TO LOOK HARD AND PERCEIVE ALL THE TECHNICAL DETAILS OF SOMETHING BEFORE YOU PUT DOWN THE LINES TO MAKE SURE YOU GET IT RIGHT. IT'S INFINITELY CHALLENGING TO DRAW FROM LIFE. THE RAPIDOGRAPH IS A SLOW DRAWING TOOL. THE LINE HAS THE LOOK OF AN ENGRAVING. I ALWAYS USED THE RAPIDOGRAPH BECAUSE IT WAS PORTABLE. WHEN I WORKED IN INK THEN, I DID NOT MAKE CORRECTIONS. THE LINE HAD TO BE RIGHT THE FIRST TIME. I GOT PRETTY GOOD AT IT. THE SKETCHBOOK WAS MY CONSTANT COMPANION. IT WAS ALWAYS WAITING FOR ME TO FILL IT. KEEPING A SKETCHBOOK CULTIVATES GOOD ARTIST VISION. IT'S REALLY A GOOD THING TO ACCUMULATE AND BUILD UP AN IDEA BANK. THE SKETCHBOOKS ARE A KIND OF COMBINATION JOURNAL AND DRAWING BOOK ... ALL PURPOSE. I'VE KIND OF LOST THAT HABIT OF LATE, UNFORTUNATELY.

THE THRUST OF MY CARTOONS THEN WAS SORT OF JULES FEIFFER INTELLECTUAL. I WAS WORKING ON TRYING TO CREATE CHARACTERS WHICH WERE SOCIAL COMMENTARIES. I MADE FRITZ THE CAT INTO A WACKY YOUNG SIXTIES UPSTART WHO WAS TRYING TO LIVE UP TO THE JACK KEROUAC IDEAL OF THE HIPSTER ON THE ROAD ... BUT HE WAS A LITTLE BIT TOO MIDDLE CLASS. HE WAS JUST A DREAMER. I WAS SATIRIZING THE ATTITUDE OF MANY YOUNG PROTO-HIPPIES EMBODIED IN A GUY LIKE RICHARD FARINA. *FRITZ THE CAT* HADN'T BEEN PUBLISHED YET, BUT I SHOWED IT TO A FEW FRIENDS AND THEY LIKED IT. IT HAD AN APPEAL TO THE HIP COLLEGE TYPES.

WHEN I TOOK LSD ... IT WAS THE *ROAD TO DAMASCUS* FOR ME! IT COMPLETELY KNOCKED ME OFF MY HORSE AND ALTERED THE WAY I DREW, THE ARRANGEMENT OF MY EGO, WHY I DREW. I STOPPED DRAWING FROM LIFE. I SORT OF LOST CONCENTRATION. I BECAME DETACHED FROM THE WHOLE EGO-INVOLVEMENT WITH CARTOONING SOMEWHAT. LSD LIBERATED ME FROM MY EGO FOR A BRIEF PERIOD. ALL MY DRAWING CAME FROM INSIDE ... AN INNER ... A MIRACULOUS VISION. IT WAS THE MOST FREE MY SUBCONSCIOUS HAS BEEN IN MY LIFE. FROM NOVEMBER '65 TO APRIL OF '66, I WAS EGOLESS, DRIFTING ALONG, TOTALLY PASSIVE. ABOUT THE ONLY THING I COULD DO WAS JUST DRAW IN MY SKETCHBOOK. IT WAS WHILE

I WAS IN THIS FUZZY STATE THAT I TOLD MY WIFE, DANA, I WAS LEAVING. I JUST WALKED OUT AND LEFT EVERYTHING. I WENT TO CHICAGO AND STAYED WITH MARTY PAHLS. I REMEMBER WANDERING AROUND CHICAGO ON THE PUBLIC BUS AIMLESSLY. MY MIND WOULD DRIFT INTO THESE CRACKLY GROTESQUE CARTOON IMAGES ACCOMPANIED BY OFF-KEY TINNY MUSIC. IT WAS IN MY BRAIN. I HAD NO CONTROL. *NO* CONTROL ... WHICH WAS GOOD FOR THE ART.

IT WAS DURING THIS STRANGE PERIOD THAT I CAME UP WITH ALL THESE CHARACTERS: MR. NATURAL, THE VULTURE DEMONESSES, EGGS ACKLEY, MR. SNOID ... I WAS SITTING AROUND MARTY PAHLS'S HOUSE ONE DAY, AND THE RADIO WAS PLAYING THIS BLACK INSTRUMENTAL JIVE MOTOWN THING. WHEN IT WAS OVER, THE ANNOUNCER SAID, "THAT WAS MR. NATURAL!" SO I DREW THIS LITTLE PUNY COMIC STRIP ABOUT A GURU TYPE WITH A BEARD TELLING THIS PERSON WHO COMES IN ASKING, "MR. NATURAL, WHAT SHOULD I DO?," "GO POLISH YOUR SHOES, BUNKY!" FOR SOME REASON, THIS FUZZY LSD FOCUSED ME IN ON THIS BIGFOOT THING. THE CHARACTERS' HEADS GOT SMALLER AND SMALLER, AND THEIR FEET GOT BIGGER AND BIGGER! I THINK SOMEHOW THIS SYMBOLIZED MY EGOLESS STATE. IT WAS ALL SO DUMB AND SO DELIBERATELY UNINTELLECTUAL! THIS WAS ANOTHER REVELATION! CARTOONS WERE JUST THESE DUMB DRAWINGS OF DUMB GUYS WITH BIG SHOES. I STARTED DRAWING THINGS MAKING FUN OF CARTOONING AND THE WHOLE LOW-BROW ENTERTAINMENT ASPECT OF CULTURE GOING BACK TO THE TWENTIES. CARTOONS WERE VERY WORKING CLASS, CHEAP AMUSEMENT FOR THE MASSES, LIKE VAUDEVILLE, EARLY MOVIES, PULP MAGAZINES AND SO ON. I MADE A DRAWING OF TWO VAUDEVILLE TYPES TELLING BAD JOKES WHILE GOING THROUGH SOME DANCE STEPS ON A STAGE. MY FRIEND MARTY PAHLS THOUGHT IT WAS FUNNY. HE POINTED OUT THAT THEY WERE "TRUCKIN'!" "KEEP ON TRUCKIN'" WAS AN OLD SONG AND AND DANCE FROM THE MID-THIRTIES THAT CAME OUT OF BLACK CULTURE. THAT TURNED INTO MY "KEEP ON TRUCKIN'" CARTOON IN *ZAP #1* THAT CAPTURED THE PUBLIC IMAGINATION AND CONTINUES TO PLAGUE ME TO THIS DAY! OH MAN, WHAT A NIGHTMARE THAT CAUSED ME! I DID MORE CARTOONS USING OLD SONG TITLES: "DUCKS YAS YAS" IS A COMPLETELY SURREAL BLACK TUNE FROM THE TWENTIES. "I'M A DING DONG DADDY" IS A WACKY NONSENSE SONG THAT CAME OUT IN THAT SAME PERIOD. IT CAME OUT OF A DRINKING CULTURE. IN THE TWENTIES, PEOPLE WERE DRUNK ALL THE TIME. THEY ALSO USED A LOT OF COCAINE, OPIUM, MORPHINE AND OTHER BAD SUBSTANCES. IT WAS A VERY WILD TIME.

THE LSD THING WAS THE MAIN BIG INSPIRATION OF MY LIFE. IT WAS AN INTENSELY VISIONARY PERIOD FOR ME. MY FACE WAS JUST VIOLENTLY PUSHED INTO THE VISIONS BY THE DRUG. YOU CAN'T CREATE THAT ARTIFICIALLY.

*Opposite*, unpublished *Zap Comix* cover, 1967; right, from *Head Comix*, 1968

"Head Comix,"
*Yarrowstalks* no. 3, 1967

"Mr. Natural" and "Big
Freakout on Detroit Ave.,"
*Yarrowstalks* no. 3, 1967

"Life Among the
Constipated,"
*Yarrowstalks* no. 3, 1967

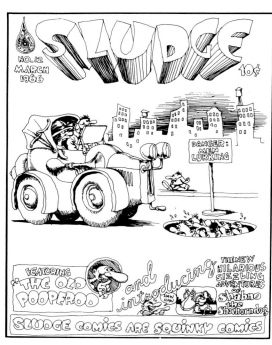

*this page and opposite*, Might-have-been comics: Crumb continuously spun out ideas for comics in his sketchbooks.

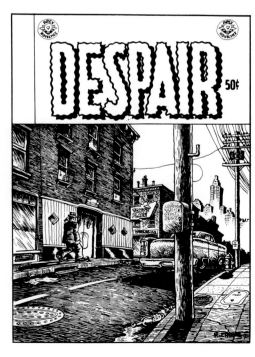

# "I DREW THE FIRST TWO ISSUES OF ZAP COMIX IN LATE 1967!"

I DREW ONE ISSUE IN OCTOBER AND ONE IN NOVEMBER. THEY WERE 24 PAGES EACH. IT WENT FAST. I SENT THE ARTWORK FOR THE FIRST ONE TO BRIAN ZAHN AND NEVER HEARD FROM HIM AGAIN. FORTUNATELY, I HAD MADE XEROXES FOR WILLIAM COLE, THIS GUY IN NEW YORK WHO WAS TALKING ABOUT DOING *HEAD COMIX* FOR VIKING PRESS. HE WANTED TO SEE XEROXES OF THIS NEW COMIC I WAS WORKING ON. DON DONAHUE SAW THE ORIGINAL ART FOR *ZAP* AND REALLY LIKED IT. DONAHUE KNEW CHARLES PLYMELL, AN OLD HIPSTER POET WHO HAD A SMALL OFFSET PRINTING PRESS, A MULTILITH 1250. DONAHUE PAID FOR THE FIRST PRINTING OF *ZAP* BY TRADING HIS $300 TAPE RECORDER TO PLYMELL IN EARLY 1968. THE FIRST PRINT RUN OF 5,000 COPIES CAME OUT. THE FIRST EDITION HAD AN ORANGE AND BLUE COVER, AND THE COVER PRICE WAS 25¢. DANA AND I, DONAHUE AND SOME FRIENDS OF OURS SOLD *ZAP* ON THE STREET AND TOOK IT AROUND TO ALL THE SHOPS ON HAIGHT STREET. THE PEOPLE WHO RAN THE HIPPIE SHOPS LOOKED AT *ZAP* AND SAID, "COMIC? WHAT DO WE WANT WITH A COMIC BOOK?" *ZAP* DIDN'T LOOK LIKE SOMETHING FROM THE HIPPIE COUNTERCULTURE ... IT LOOKED LIKE AN ORDINARY COMIC BOOK. WE JUST KEPT PUSHING IT, AND PEOPLE FINALLY GOT THE IDEA THERE WAS SOMETHING PSYCHEDELIC ABOUT IT. THE FIRST PRINTING SOLD OUT IN A FEW MONTHS, AND DONAHUE REPRINTED ANOTHER 5,000 COPIES, WITH AN INCREASE IN THE PRICE TO 35¢.

SHORTLY AFTER *ZAP #1* CAME OUT, DONAHUE BROUGHT S. CLAY WILSON OVER TO MY HOUSE WANTING TO COLLABORATE ON SOMETHING. HE HAD JUST COME OUT FROM KANSAS, SEEN *ZAP #1* AND WANTED TO SHOW ME HIS WORK. I ADMIRED HIS STUFF AND WAS HAPPY TO COLLABORATE WITH HIM. I HAD ALSO ADMIRED RICK GRIFFIN AND VICTOR MOSCOSO'S PSYCHEDELIC POSTERS, AND THEY SAW *ZAP*, LIKED IT AND SOMEHOW WE ALL ENDED UP WORKING TOGETHER — THE FOUR OF US — ON THE SECOND ISSUE OF *ZAP*. VICTOR TOOK THE LEAD IN ORGANIZING THE BUSINESS END, HOOKED US UP WITH THE LAWYER MICHAEL STEPANIAN AND PUT THINGS IN WRITING. I WAS HAPPY WITH THAT AND APPRECIATED VICTOR'S BUSINESS ACUMEN. WE CALLED OUR COLLECTIVE OWNERSHIP "APEX NOVELTIES" AFTER THIS LITTLE TAG I HAD PUT ON THE COVER OF *ZAP #1* AS A JOKE.

FOR THE THIRD ISSUE OF *ZAP*, GILBERT SHELTON AND SPAIN RODRIGUEZ WERE INVITED TO PARTICIPATE. I HAD BEEN IMMEDIATELY STRUCK BY SPAIN'S WORK WHEN I FIRST SAW IT, AND I HAD BEEN AWARE OF AND ADMIRED GILBERT'S WORK SINCE I HAD SEEN IT IN *THE TEXAS RANGER* CIRCA 1964~65. OF COURSE, WILSON, GRIFFIN AND MOSCOSO'S APPROVAL WAS NEEDED FOR ANY ARTIST TO BE LET IN. ALSO IT WAS AT THIS TIME I TOLD THE OTHER *ZAP* ARTISTS ABOUT SENDING A COMPLETE BOOK OFF TO BRIAN ZAHN AND NEVER GETTING WORD OR ART BACK. THEY TOLD ME I HAD TO GET THE ART BACK AND GET THIS PRINTED. I COULDN'T TRACK BRIAN ZAHN DOWN, BUT I REMEMBERED THE XEROXES I HAD SENT TO WILLIAM

COLE. I CONTACTED HIM AND REQUESTED THE XEROXES, WHICH I HAD TO DOCTOR, AND I HAD TO REDRAW THE COVER SINCE THIS BOOK HAD BEEN DRAWN BEFORE WHAT WAS NOW KNOWN AS *ZAP #1*.

IT BECAME *ZAP #0*. TEN YEARS LATER, MY LAWYER ALBERT MORSE GOT THE ORIGINAL ART BACK FROM ZAHN, BUT I ONLY SAW IT BRIEFLY BEFORE IT DISAPPEARED AGAIN. THAT COMIC HAS NEVER YET BEEN PRINTED FROM THE ORIGINAL ARTWORK.

THEN WITH THE FOURTH ISSUE, ROBERT WILLIAMS WAS BROUGHT IN. THIS WAS AROUND LATE 1969, I BELIEVE. EVERYONE IN THE *ZAP* "COLLECTIVE" LIKED AND ADMIRED HIS WORK, AND IT WAS AGREED TO HAVE HIM AS A PARTNER IN THE GROUP. WITH HIS INCLUSION, THE *ZAP* GANG WAS "COMPLETE." THE "MAGNIFICENT SEVEN," THE KICK-ASS SEVEN *ZAP* ARTISTS, THE BADDEST GANG OF CARTOONISTS EVER TO WIELD THEIR CROWQUILLS TOGETHER ... THAT'S HOW WE SAW OURSELVES, SILLY BOYS THAT WE WERE.

BY THE FOURTH ISSUE, THOUGH, THE BOOK WAS IN A PATTERN OF NOT GETTING AN ISSUE COMPLETED MORE THAN ONCE A YEAR. VERY EARLY ON, I FOUND THIS A BIT FRUSTRATING, BUT I COULD ACCEPT IT ... WE WERE THE BEST ... WE WERE LIKE A GODDAMN ROCK BAND — THE COMPLETED BOOK WAS LIKE OUR LATEST ALBUM ... IT WAS AN EVENT WHEN THE LATEST *ZAP* CAME OFF THE PRESSES. *ZAP* WAS THE MOST POPULAR AND WELL-KNOWN "UNDERGROUND" COMIC. GETTING IT OUT REGULARLY WOULD NOT ONLY HAVE HELPED THE WHOLE ALTERNATIVE COMICS BUSINESS (SUCH AS IT WAS) TO ESTABLISH ITSELF, BUT WOULD HAVE BEEN A GREAT VENUE FOR OTHER OBVIOUS TALENTS LIKE KIM DEITCH, JUSTIN GREEN AND BUCKWHEAT FLORIDA JR. THESE SUGGESTIONS WERE KIBOSHED MOST VIGOROUSLY BY MOSCOSO AND WILSON. OH WELL. IT WAS A HELL OF A GROUP OF ARTISTS ANYWAY.

I BEGAN TO LOSE INTEREST, OR PASSION, FOR *ZAP COMIX* IN THE EARLY SEVENTIES. ALREADY BY 1973, THE SEVEN OF US WERE SEEN AS "THE ESTABLISHMENT," "THE GRAND OLD MEN" OF UNDERGROUND COMIX, EXCLUDING ALL OTHERS FROM OUR LITTLE CLUB. PART OF WHAT I LOVED ABOUT THE UNDERGROUND WAS ITS LOOSE, WIDE-OPEN EXPERIMENTAL QUALITY. EVENTUALLY IT BECAME A "BONE OF CONTENTION" BETWEEN ME AND THE OTHER *ZAP* ARTISTS.

*ARCADE* CAME ALONG IN THE MID-SEVENTIES AND ATTEMPTED TO BE A RALLYING POINT FOR UNDERGROUND CARTOONISTS. A NOBLE EFFORT, BUT ART SPIEGELMAN AND BILL GRIFFITH WERE TOO "HIGH STRUNG" TO KEEP THE MAGAZINE GOING OVER THE LONG HAUL ... THEY DID MANAGE TO GET OUT SEVEN ISSUES, THOUGH, BEFORE THEY BOTH WENT CRAZY IN THE PROCESS. ARTIE WENT ON TO PRODUCE THE HIGHLY "ARTISTIC" *RAW* MAGAZINE, WHILE I WENT ON TO PRODUCE THE VERY UNARTISTIC *WEIRDO* IN 1981. *WEIRDO* HAD ITS DAY ... 27 ISSUES OVER A NINE YEAR PERIOD —— '81 TO '90 ... WE PRINTED WORK BY CERTIFIED LUNATICS, PRIMITIVES, PSYCHOPATHS, ARTISTS WHO CAME AND WENT AND SOME WHO TURNED OUT TO BE THE BEST OF THE YOUNGER GENERATION, AS WELL AS SOME OF THE "PIONEERS" OF THE OLD UNDERGROUND.

*opposite*, sketchbook drawing, 1992; *above*, back cover of Zap Comix no. 2 (detail), 1968

"Mr. Sketchum is at it Again!" *Zap Comix* no. 0, 1967

"Keep on Truckin' . . ."
*Zap Comix* no. 1, 1967

"Av 'n' Gar," *The East Village*
*Other* vol. 3, no. 1, 1967

One of Crumb's
two rock posters,
1967

"Schuman the Human," *The East Village Other* vol. 3, no. 10, 1968

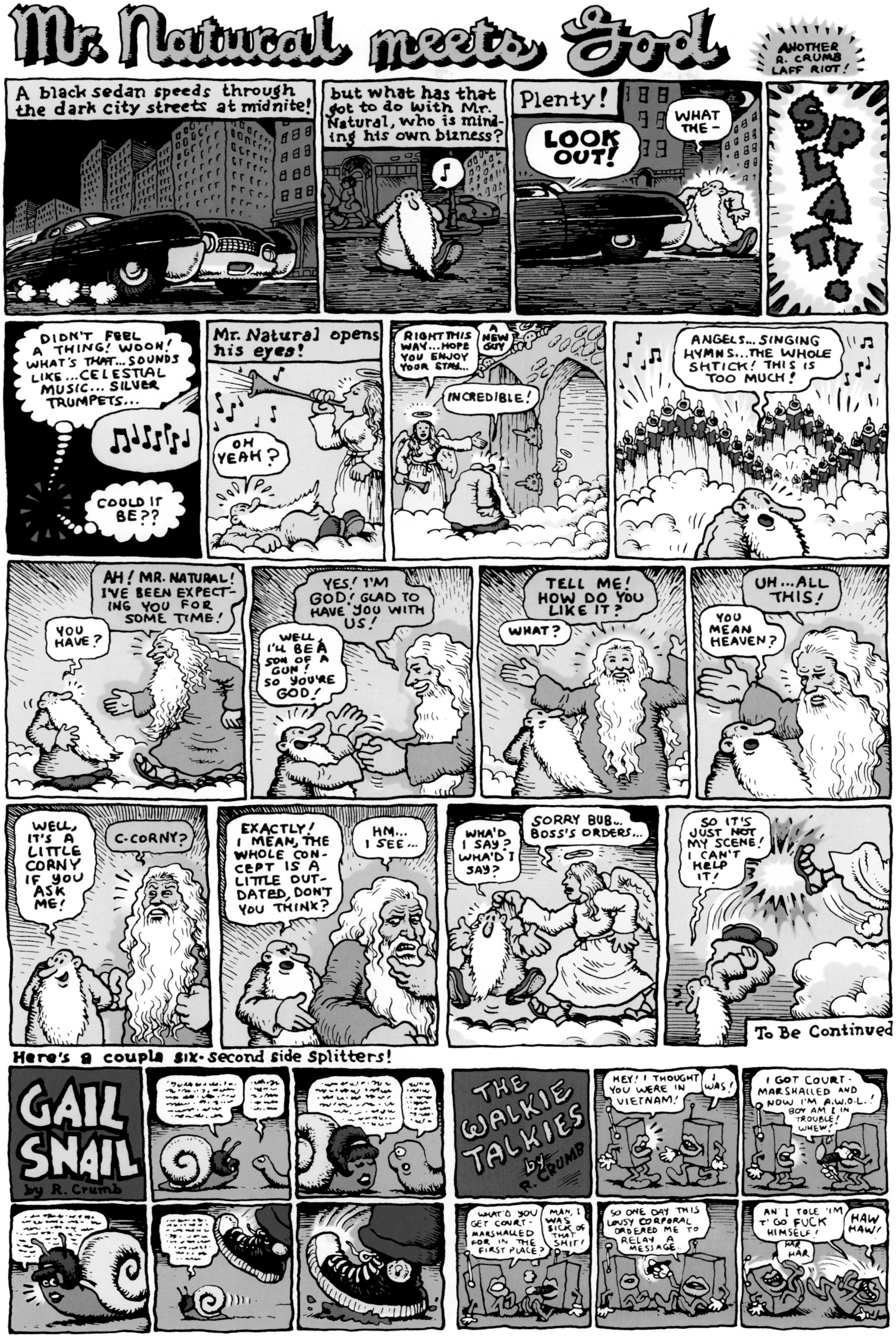


"Mr. Natural Meets God," *The East Village Other* vol. 3, no. 11, 1968

"Mr. Natural gets the bum's rush" and
"Let's Be Honest," *The East Village
Other* vol. 3, no. 12, 1968

"Mr. Natural Repents," *The East Village Other* vol. 3, no. 13, 1968

# "I WAS VERY ALIENATED FROM THE HIPPIE SCENE! I USED TO GO TO LOVE-INS AND ROCK CONCERTS AND THINK, 'WHY CAN'T I GET WITH IT?'"

I WAS STILL UNKNOWN, IGNORED AND LONELY. WHY COULDN'T I CUT LOOSE, KICK OFF MY SHOES AND DANCE IN THE GRASS...WEAR PATCHOULI OIL... LOVE BEADS... DIG THE GRATEFUL DEAD? I JUST COULDN'T GET WITH THAT PROGRAM AT ALL. I MEAN... I WAS THERE. I BELIEVED IN A LOT OF THE SAME THINGS. I WAS CARRIED ALONG ON THE WAVE OF OPTIMISM. I WAS SYMPATHETIC TO IT, BUT I WAS JUST TOO PHYSICALLY AND EMOTIONALLY INHIBITED TO BE A HIPPIE. I EVEN HAD AN INTELLECTUAL CRITICISM OF THE WHOLE THING TO A DEGREE, BUT I, TOO, BELIEVED THAT THE WORLD WAS PERMANENTLY CHANGED, THAT AS SOON AS THE OLD FARTS DIED OFF IT WAS GOING TO BE A BETTER PLACE. I ALSO SAW THAT A LOT OF IT WAS JUST EXCESSIVE. PEOPLE WERE BUYING INTO THE HIPPIE STYLE AND ETHIC WHOLESALE WHO WERE COMPLETELY UNCRITICAL. THEN THEY WOULD BE "HIPPER THAN THOU" ABOUT IT AND GO A-ROUND JUDGING PEOPLE BY HOW "TURNED ON" THEY WERE. THERE WAS A LOT OF SPIRITUAL NONSENSE AS WELL AS LEFT-WING NONSENSE. CAN YOU IMAGINE IF PEOPLE LIKE ELDRIDGE CLEAVER OR ABBIE HOFFMAN HAD ACTUALLY GOTTEN INTO POWER? JEEZIS! IT'S FRIGHTENING! THERE WOULD HAVE BEEN PRISON CAMPS FULL OF PEOPLE NOT HIP ENOUGH AND PRISON GUARDS WITH BIG PEACE SYMBOLS ON THEIR ARM BANDS.

IT STILL AMAZES ME HOW ENTHUSIASTICALLY THE EDITORS OF UNDERGROUND PAPERS RESPONDED TO MY STUFF: "OH YEAH! THIS IS GREAT! GIVE US MORE!" OF COURSE, IN THE BEGINNING, THERE WAS NO MONEY. I DON'T THINK MANY PEOPLE GOT PAID...PROBABLY THE PERMANENT STAFF... ALL OF THREE PEOPLE. THEY PAID THEMSELVES SOMETHING. BUT THE UNDERGROUND NEWSPAPERS WERE PRODUCED ON A SHOESTRING BUDGET. THE OFFICE OF *THE EAST VILLAGE OTHER* IN NEW YORK WAS QUITE A SCENE — FREELOADERS HANGING AROUND, SLEEPING ON A COUCH OR IN A BACK ROOM, ALWAYS LOTS OF CUTE YOUNG GIRLS AND THERE WAS A LOT OF DOPE BEING SMOKED ALL THE TIME. PEOPLE WOULD TAKE LSD ON PASTE-UP NIGHT AT *THE EAST VILLAGE OTHER*. THE OFFICE WAS A FUN PLACE TO HANG OUT — PEOPLE WERE RUNNING IN AND OUT. IT WAS EXCITING. THEY WOULD PRINT ANYTHING THAT WAS HALFWAY READABLE. THERE WAS NO CENSORSHIP. I COULD HAND IN A PAGE LIKE "PHONUS BALONUS BLUES" OR "ALL ASSHOLE COMICS," AND NOBODY WOULD BLINK. THEY WOULD RUN IT HAVING BARELY LOOKED AT IT. BY 1967, THEY WERE HAPPY TO PRINT ANYTHING OUTRAGEOUS! *PORNO CHIC* CAME OUT OF THAT, AROUND '69 OR '70. *SCREW* IS STILL GOING. YOU COULD DO WHOLE TABLOID-SIZE PAGES OR EVEN COVERS FOR *THE EAST VILLAGE OTHER*. WOW! IT DIDN'T PAY ANYTHING, BUT IT WAS ON THE NEWSSTANDS A FEW DAYS AFTER YOU DREW IT. THAT'S A LOT OF POWER! YOU WERE REALLY FLEXING YOUR ARTISTIC MUSCLES FILLING UP THOSE NEWSPAPERS. GENERALLY YOU GOT YOUR ARTWORK BACK. SOMETIMES THINGS WERE STOLEN OR MISPLACED.

WHEN I WAS LIVING IN SAN FRANCISCO, I HAD SENT SOME STRIPS IN TO A PAPER CALLED *YARROWSTALKS* PUBLISHED BY A GUY IN PHILADELPHIA, BRIAN ZAHN. IT WAS PRINTED ON GOOD WHITE PAPER STOCK AND FULL OF GOD-AWFUL HIPPIE ARTWORK AND LONG-WINDED TREATISES ON EASTERN RELIGION. ZAHN CAME TO SEE ME AND ASKED IF I WOULD LIKE TO DO A COMPLETE ISSUE, SO I DREW THE WHOLE ISSUE OF *YARROWSTALKS #3*. MOST OF THE STUFF WAS JUST REDRAWN COMIC STRIPS OUT OF MY SKETCHBOOKS. IT WAS THE CONVERGENCE OF A WHOLE LOT OF THINGS AND REFLECTED THE PEAK OF THE HIPPIE ERA. THE HIPPIES LIKED IT, AND IT WAS THE BEGINNING OF MY BECOMING A COUNTER-CULTURE HERO. ZAHN THEN SUGGESTED I DO A WHOLE COMIC BOOK WHICH HE WOULD PUBLISH. AFTER MY "ON THE ROAD" EXPERIENCE DURING THE "SUMMER OF LOVE," I RETURNED TO SAN FRANCISCO AND RESOLVED TO GET TO WORK. AND THAT'S WHEN I DREW THE FIRST TWO ISSUES OF *ZAP COMIX*.

THEN THE "LOVE" STARTED TO HAPPEN TO ME. IT WAS 1968. PEOPLE FROM AROUND THE HAIGHT-ASHBURY "NEIGHBORHOOD" STARTED COMING AROUND...JANIS JOPLIN AND OTHER MEMBERS OF BIG BROTHER AND THE HOLDING COMPANY. JANIS LIKED *ZAP COMIX* AND *SNATCH COMIX*. MY COMICS APPEALED TO THE HARD-DRINKING, HARD-FUCKING END OF THE HIPPIE SPECTRUM AS OPPOSED TO THE SPIRITUAL, EASTERN-RELIGIOUS, LIGHTER-THAN-AIR TYPE OF HIPPIE. JANIS ASKED ME TO DO AN ALBUM COVER. I WAS FLATTERED, BUT I WASN'T CRAZY ABOUT THE MUSIC. I LIKED JANIS OK AND I DID THE COVER. I TOOK SPEED AND DID AN ALL-NIGHTER. THE FRONT COVER I DESIGNED WASN'T USED AT ALL. THEY USED THE BACK COVER FOR THE FRONT. I GOT PAID $600. THE ALBUM COVER IMPRESSED THE HELL OUT OF GIRLS MUCH MORE SO THAN THE COMICS. I GOT A LOT OF MILEAGE OUT OF THAT OVER THE YEARS! VIKING WANTED TO DO A BOOK OF MY WORK. *HEAD COMIX* CAME OUT...THEN *FRITZ THE CAT*. THINGS STARTED TO HAPPEN THICK AND FAST WITH FRITZ, AND SLEAZY HUSTLING BUSINESSMEN WANTED TO EXPLOIT THE CHARACTER. IT WAS A NEW BALLGAME FOR ME, KIND OF SCARY. THERE WAS THIS ONE GROUP OF GUYS WHO PAID MY WAY TO NEW YORK AND WANTED ME TO SIGN AN EXCLUSIVE FIVE-YEAR CONTRACT. THEY WERE GUYS IN LEATHER TRENCH COATS WHO GOT REALLY ANNOYED WHEN I LAUGHED AT THEM. I WAS NAIVE BUT LUCKILY NOT STUPID ENOUGH TO SIGN SOMETHING LIKE THAT. THESE OLDER BUSINESSMEN TYPES WERE TRYING TO CASH IN JUST AS FAST AS THEY COULD ON THE "HIPPIE PHENOMENON." THEY WERE ALL OVER IT LOOKING FOR ANGLES, MONEY-MAKING POSSIBILITIES.

IN 1968-69, AS I TRAVERSED DIFFERENT CITIES, I NOTICED THESE "COMICS SCENES" STARTING UP. I DIDN'T KNOW JAY LYNCH UNTIL HE SENT ME *BIJOU FUNNIES*, BUT WHEN I WENT TO CHICAGO IN '68, HE, SKIP WILLIAMSON AND JAY KINNEY ALREADY HAD A COMICS SCENE GOING, THE BIJOU PUBLISHING EMPIRE. I MET SPAIN RODRIGUEZ AND KIM DEITCH IN NEW YORK; THEY WERE DOING COMICS ON A REGULAR BASIS FOR *THE EAST VILLAGE OTHER*. ANN ARBOR HAD SOMETHING HAPPENING. EVERY COLLEGE CAMPUS HAD ITS OWN LITTLE HIP SCENE IN THOSE DAYS, USUALLY INVOLVING SOME KIND OF MUSIC NONSENSE, COFFEE HOUSES, "UNDERGROUND"-STYLE PAPERS, AND SOMETIMES COMICS. AND ALWAYS, THE DRUGS.

I REMEMBER IN 1970 WORRYING WHETHER I WAS PART OF THE SOLUTION OR PART OF THE PROBLEM. ELDRIDGE CLEAVER HAD SAID YOU WERE ONE OR THE OTHER. I HAD A LOT OF ANXIETY ABOUT IT... GEE... WHICH AM I? I DON'T KNOW. I NEVER DID DECIDE. LATER IT BECAME A MOOT POINT. THINGS WERE NOT AS SIMPLE AS WE'D THOUGHT THEY WERE, UNFORTUNATELY ... OR FORTUNATELY.

*opposite, cover of Cheap Thrills, 1968*

*opposite*, cover of *R. Crumb's Fritz the Cat*, 1969; *this page*, "All Asshole Comics," *Chicago Seed* vol. 3, no. 1, 1968

97

cover and "The Phonus Balonus Blues," *The East Village Other* vol. 3, no. 43, 1968

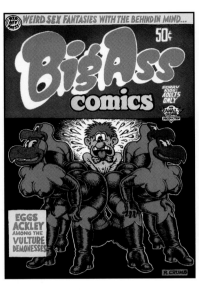

"Artsy Fartsy," *Big Ass Comics*
no. 1, 1969

# STONED AGIN!

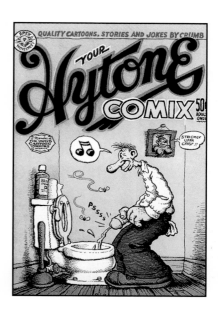

"Stoned Agin!" Your
Hytone Comix, 1971

"The Lighter-Than-Air Boys," *Plunge into the Depths of Despair*, 1970

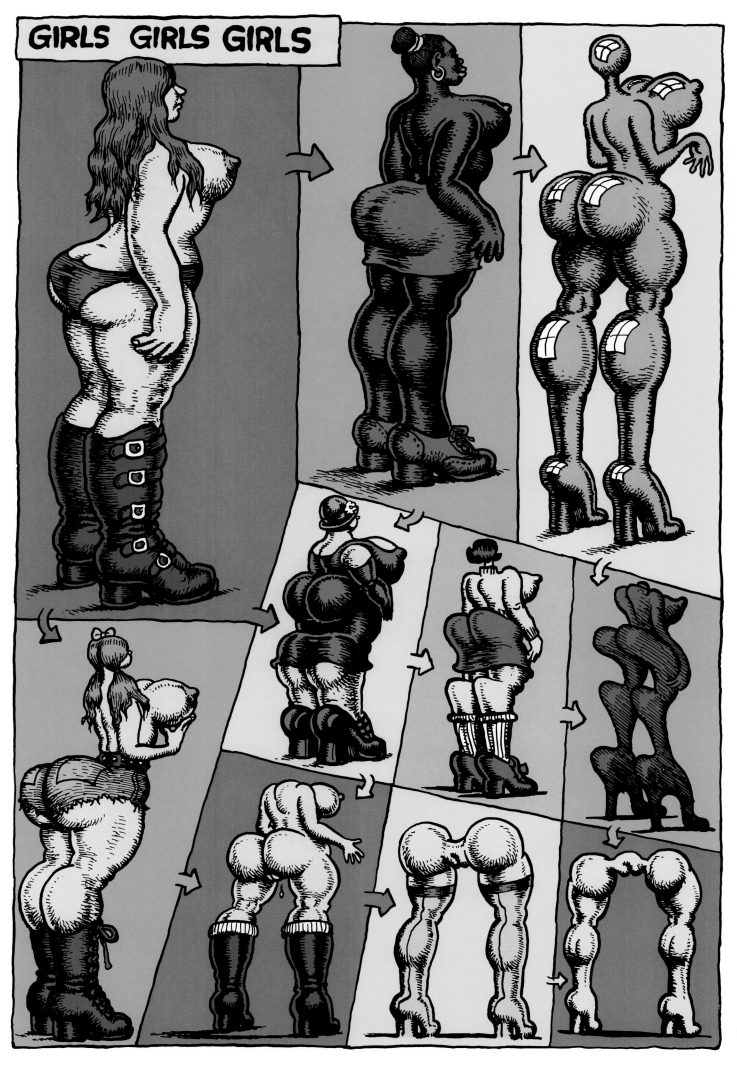
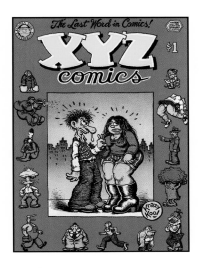

"Girls Girls Girls," *XYZ Comics*, 1972

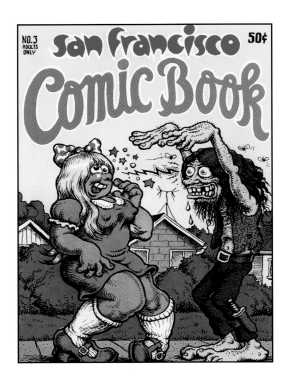

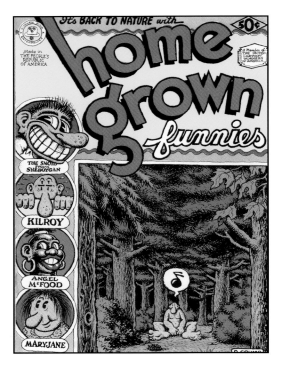

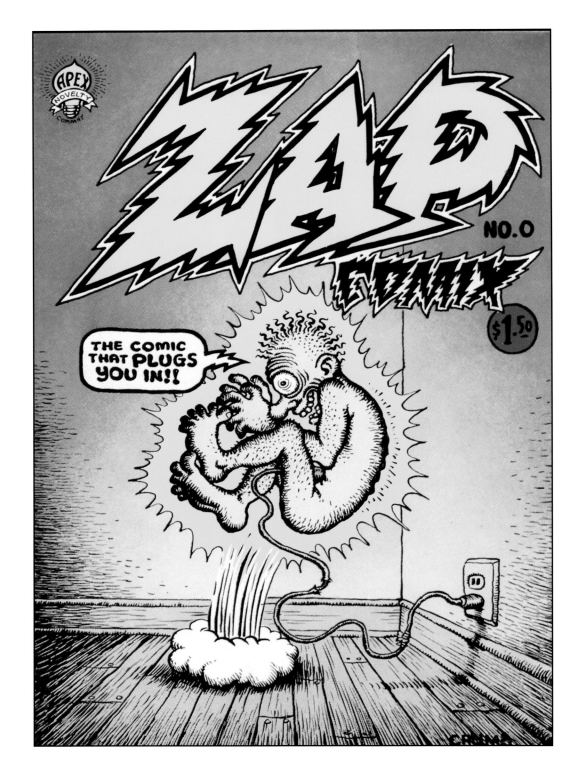

this page, clockwise from the top right,
Zap Comix no. 0, 1967; Black and White
Comics, 1973; Motor City Comics no. 1,
1969; Home Grown Funnies, 1971;
San Francisco Comic Book no. 3, 1970;
opposite page, clockwise from top left, Zap
Comix no. 1, 1967; Uneeda Comix, 1970;
R. Crumb's Best Buy Comics, 1979; Snoid
Comics, 1980; Mr. Natural no. 1, 1970;
The People's Comics, 1972

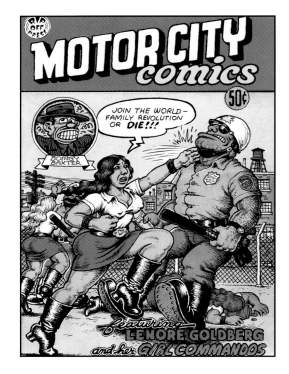

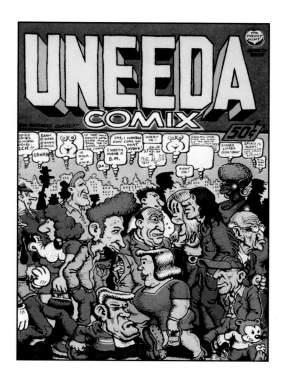

# "MY PERSONAL OBSESSION FOR BIG WOMEN INTERFERES WITH SOME PEOPLE'S ENJOYMENT OF MY WORK!"

SOME FIND IT INTERESTING, BUT TO SEE IT OVER AND OVER AGAIN... I HAVE QUALMS ABOUT THAT, BUT ONCE IT WAS OUT OF THE BAG, I COULDN'T SEEM TO STOP IT.

I STARTED DRAWING SEXY WOMEN THE FIRST TIME MY BROTHER CHARLES LEFT HOME FOR SIX WEEKS. I WAS 17 AT THE TIME. BEFORE THAT, I COULDN'T DO IT. I FELT TOO INHIBITED, BUT WITH HIM NOT LOOKING OVER MY SHOULDER, I SUDDENLY BURST FORTH WITH ALL THESE FEMALE FANTASIES ON PAPER. THEN CHARLES CAME BACK AND LOOKED THROUGH MY DRAWINGS.

"WHAT ARE ALL THESE WOMEN YOU'RE DRAWING? WHY DO THEY ALL HAVE BIG LEGS? WHAT IS THIS? WHAT IS THIS ALL ABOUT?" IT WAS EMBARRASSING, BUT AT THIS POINT, THERE WAS NO TURNING BACK. CHARLES SAW IT. I ENDURED HIS GAZE OF RIDICULE AND SARCASM AND WENT ON MY WAY. IN MY YOUTH, I WAS AN OBSESSED PATHETIC CREEP CUT OFF FROM THE OUTSIDE WORLD, AND IN THE PROCESS, I DEVELOPED THESE STRANGE, VERY INDIVIDUALISTIC SEX FANTASIES. SO IT GOES.

I'VE BEEN TRYING TO RESOLVE THE SEX OBSESSION WITH THE ART THING FOR MY WHOLE LIFE. WHEN I SAW THE WORK OF S. CLAY WILSON IN THE SUMMER OF '68, IT WAS A REVELATION TO ME. WILSON DREW ANY CRAZY IDEA THAT CAME INTO HIS HEAD, NO MATTER HOW TWISTED OR VIOLENT OR SEXUALLY WEIRD OR WHATEVER. HE JUST DREW IT. I THOUGHT, "YEAH, WHY STOP YOURSELF? JUST PUT IT ALL OUT THERE AND SEE WHAT HAPPENS." ONE TIME I WAS TELLING WILSON THAT I WAS UNCERTAIN ABOUT DOING CARTOONS FOR MASS CONSUMPTION AND WHETHER OR NOT ONE SHOULD WORRY ABOUT BEING ENTERTAINING. WILSON SAID, "CRUMB, DOING WORK TO ENTERTAIN THE MASSES IS JUST FEEDING THE HUNGRY DOG!" WILSON ALSO THOUGHT MY WORK HAD TOO MUCH CUTENESS, LEFT OVER FROM MY AMERICAN GREETINGS DAYS.

WELL, AS THE BIBLE SAYS IN MARK 4:22 (QUOTING JESUS), "FOR THERE IS NOTHING HID WHICH SHALL NOT BE MANIFESTED; NEITHER WAS ANYTHING KEPT SECRET BUT THAT IT SHOULD COME ABROAD." THERE ARE NO SECRETS FROM GOD. SECRET SEX FANTASIES? OH WELL, MIGHT AS WELL PUT IT ALL DOWN ON PAPER! AT FIRST, IT WASN'T DEEPLY PERSONAL, BUT AS I WENT ALONG IT BECAME MORE AND MORE SO. IT STARTED TO BOTHER ME. DOES THE WORLD REALLY WANT TO KNOW THIS? I KNEW IT WAS WEIRD AND DISTURBING AND EVEN OFFENSIVE TO A LOT OF PEOPLE, PARTICULARLY WOMEN. BUT I COULDN'T KEEP IT OUT OF THE COMICS. I WOULD ALWAYS TRY TO GIVE IT SOME SORT OF METAPHORICAL SENSE BECAUSE I DERIVED SUCH MASTURBATORY PLEASURE OUT OF DRAWING THESE WOMEN IN BIZARRE SITUATIONS WITH THESE LITTLE GUYS DOING STUFF TO THEM. I REALLY ENJOYED THAT. I HAD TO DO IT. IT WAS ADDICTING! I WAS HOOKED!

JUST IN TIME, TOO! HERE COME TH' REST OF THE LADYBIRD-DEMONS!!

*opposite*, Racial Stereotype: sketchbook page, late '60s; *center*, panel from "Eggs Ackley Among the Vulture Demonesses," *Big Ass Comics* no. 1, 1969

I HAD A HARD TIME CONTROLLING IT, AND I GRAPPLED WITH IT FOR 30 YEARS. SOMETIMES, I HAVE HAD TWINGES OF REGRET BECAUSE ONCE THIS STUFF IS OUT THERE, YOU HAVE TO LIVE WITH IT. IT HAUNTS YOU THE REST OF YOUR FUCKING LIFE, AND PEOPLE WILL COME BACK AT YOU POINTING OUT SIMILARITIES BETWEEN A SEXUAL FANTASY I DID IN 1969 IN *BIG ASS COMICS*, WHEN EGGS ACKLEY STUFFED THE VULTURE DEMONESS'S HEAD UP HER ASS, AND A THING I DID IN 1992 WITH MR. NATURAL AND THE DEVIL GIRL. "OH YEAH! I GUESS I DID!" YOU HAVE TO LIVE WITH THAT STUFF! IT'S TOUGH! IT'S LIKE HAVING YOUR BODY TATTOOED FROM HEAD TO FOOT. YOU CAN'T ERASE IT!... OVER HERE IS EGGS ACKLEY AND THE VULTURE DEMONESSES, AND OVER HERE IS DEVIL GIRL. I'M MARKED FOR LIFE, BRANDED WITH MY OWN NUTTY CREATIONS! OH BOY...

SIMILARLY, USING RACIST STEREOTYPES, IT'S BOILING OVER OUT OF MY BRAIN, AND I JUST HAVE TO DRAW IT! POUR IT ON AS THICK AS I CAN AND NOT LEAVE ANY OF THE PARANOIA OUT. PUT IT ALL IN THERE. HEY, IN MY OWN DEFENSE, I AM *NOT* A RACIST! COME ON! I DON'T CONSCIOUSLY BELIEVE THAT ANY RACE IS INFERIOR TO ANY OTHER RACE. I DON'T BELIEVE THAT JEWS ARE ANY MORE SINISTER OR MORALLY CORRUPT THAN ANY OTHER PEOPLE... BUT ALL THIS STUFF IS DEEPLY EMBEDDED IN OUR CULTURE AND OUR COLLECTIVE SUBCONSCIOUS, AND YOU HAVE TO DEAL WITH IT. IT'S IN ME. IT'S IN EVERYBODY. IT'S THERE! IT'S HUMAN NATURE, DENY IT THOUGH YOU WILL. SOME PEOPLE SAY THAT THE WAY I PLAY AROUND WITH IT IS TOO ROUGH. IT HURTS PEOPLE'S FEELINGS. I SUPPOSE IT DOES. SOME PEOPLE FEEL PERSONALLY ATTACKED BY IT. A PERVERSE PART OF ME LIKES TO TAKE THE HEAT FOR ALL THAT STUFF. THEN PEOPLE CAN HATE ME AND FEEL RIGHTEOUSLY INDIGNANT ABOUT IT, BUT MEANWHILE, I'VE BROUGHT IT ALL OUT IN THE OPEN. I DON'T KNOW... IT'S WEIRD. I DON'T KNOW WHY I DO THAT. MAYBE I SHOULDN'T DO IT ANYMORE. IT MIGHT BE DANGEROUS FOR MY HEALTH. SOMEBODY EVENTUALLY IS GOING TO WANT TO HURT ME FOR DRAWING THIS STUFF. I THINK ABOUT THAT SOMETIMES.

drawing, 1969

sketchbook
page, 1975

sketchbook page, 1975

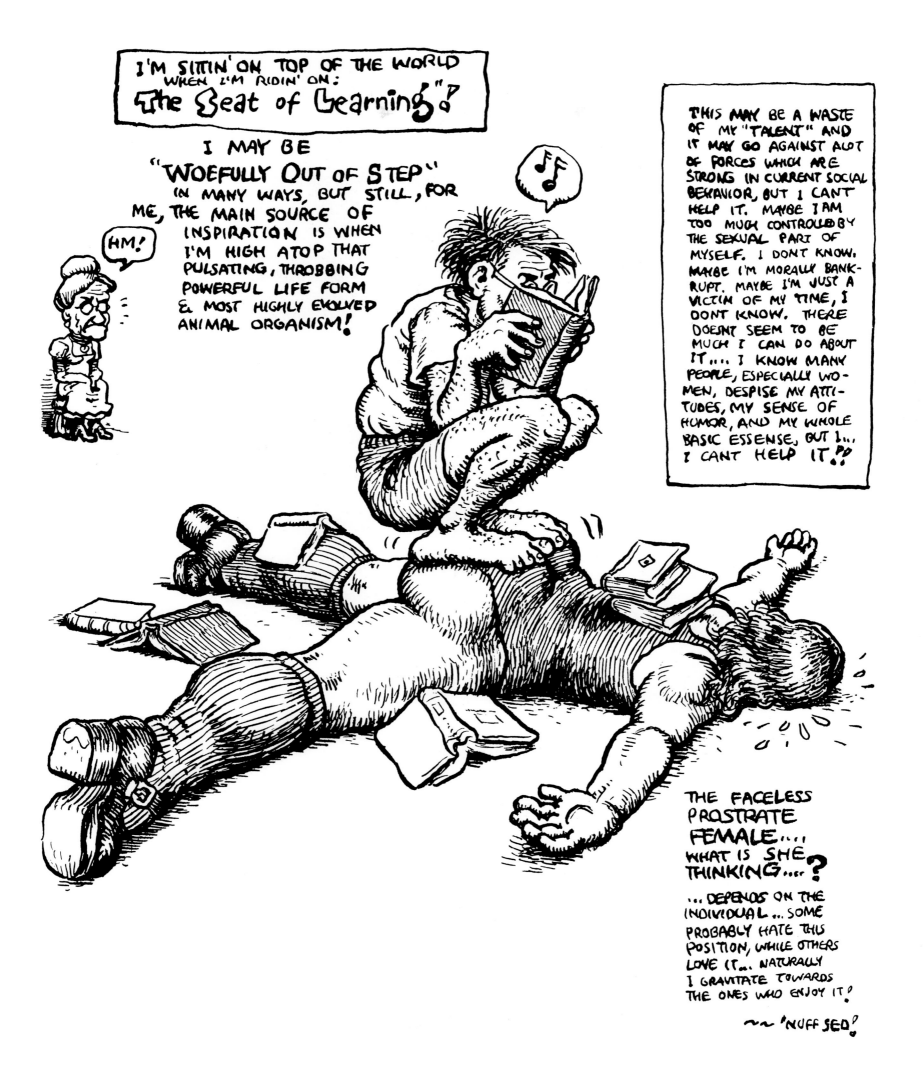

sketchbook page, 1975

"My Troubles With Women,"
*Zap Comix* no. 10, 1980

THROUGH THE REST OF MY TEEN YEARS I THOUGHT MYSELF THE MOST UNFORTUNATE SOUL ON THE FACE OF THE EARTH... SPENT HOURS BROODING OVER THE LOUSY DEAL LIFE HAD HANDED ME...

I'LL BECOME A GREAT ARTIST... THEN THEY'LL BE SORRY THEY REJECTED ME!

I DID HAVE SOME BEAUTIFUL BROODING PLACES...

PLUS, I WAS "HORNY" EVERY SECOND OF THE WAKING DAY...

WHY IS IT THAT GIRLS ALWAYS GO FOR THE MEANEST, JERKIEST GUYS??

"FONZ" TYPE

HIS RING

DOLLY HENSLEY, ONE OF MY SECRET CRUSHES

GREEN WITH ENVY →

HEY, HOW 'BOUT THOSE "HAPPY DAYS"?!

IF ONLY I KNEW THEN WHAT I KNOW NOW!!

WHATTA THEY SEE IN A BIG DUM BLOW-HARD LIKE HIM?? I'M SMARTER, KINDER, MORE INTERESTING...*

BUCKY SULLIVAN MY MOST HATED ENEMY

NECK HOLD

* I DIDN'T REALIZE YET THAT I WAS ALSO "SENSITIVE"...

GIRLS LIKED TO CONFIDE IN ME... I WAS SOMEONE WHO WAS UNDERSTANDING, SYMPATHETIC...

...HE'S SO CONCEITED, SO ARROGANT! LISTEN TO WHAT HE DID TA ME YESTIDAY!

KAREN, YOU DESERVE BETTER IN LIFE THAN THAT!

OH, ROBERT, YOU'RE SUCH A NICE BOY... I WISH I COULD TALK TO MIKE ABOUT THINGS LIKE THIS... HE WONT LISTEN TO ME... HE ALWAYS TELLS ME TO SHUT UP... HE DOESNT GIVE ME ANY CREDIT... HE'S SO CUTE, ME THIS ME THAT... BLAH BLAH YAKITY YAK...

"NICE BOY"... THAT'S ME... AND, WHERE DO "NICE" GUYS FINISH??

ANOTHER THING THAT USED TO GET MY GOAT WAS THE WAY GIRLS WOULD MOON OVER THE MOST OBNOXIOUS STRUTTING BANTY-ROOSTER ROCK STARS, MOVIE STARS, ETC.

SIGH... HE'S SO-O-O DREAMY!

ARGH!

DAN-DRUFF

HEY FRANKIE!!

FRONT TOOTH MISSING →

I'M TELLING YOU, I WAS ACQUIRING A LOW OPINION OF WOMEN!

117

BY AGE TWENTY I WAS A SEETHING SEX PERVERT WEIRDO, OBSESSED WITH SICK, TWISTED SEX FANTASIES WHICH HAD NOTHING TO DO WITH REALITY.* THE REALITY WAS THAT I HADN'T EVEN KISSED A GIRL YET! I WAS A DESPERATE MAN

*HAVEN'T CHANGED ALL THAT MUCH

THE NEXT THING I KNEW I WAS MARRIED...

MY FATHER ALWAYS SAID I'D MARRY THE FIRST ONE THAT CAME ALONG!

IT'S HARD TO SAY WHO WAS MORE NEUROTIC, ME OR HER...

ROBERT! WHERE ARE YOU GOING?? ARE YOU LEAVING ME NOW?? — SOB

IT'S OKAY! I'M JUST GOIN' TO SEE ABOUT A JOB, HONEY! HONEST! I'LL BE BACK TONIGHT! REALLY!!

THE SAD PART WAS, I REALLY WAS JUST GOING TO SEE ABOUT A JOB!

WHEW! THIS BEING MARRIED IS A LITTLE BIT SUFFOCATING!

YOUNG GO-GETTER

THEN SOMETHING AMAZING HAPPENED IN MY BLEAK LIFE...IN THE LATE 'SIXTIES I DID SOME LSD-INSPIRED "COMIX" WHICH MADE ME AN "UNDER-GROUND" CULT HERO...BEAUTIFUL YOUNG "HIPPIE CHICKS" BEGAN MAKING THEMSELVES AVAILABLE...

HI BOB...

BOB?

I COULDN'T BELIEVE THIS WAS HAPPENING TO ME! I WAS AWESTRUCK! DUMB-FOUNDED! TAKEN ABACK! HOW COULD SUCH GIRLS POSSIBLY LIKE A GAWKY GOOF LIKE ME? IT SEEMED INCONGRUOUS!

Y-YOU'RE SO BEAUTIFUL...

ULP GULP

SO I'M BEAUTIFUL, SO WHAT?!

HEY JUDE DON'T BE AFRAID TAKE A SAD SONG AND MAKE IT BETTER

121

122

123

# The Perfect Female Body

ACCORDING TO THE PERSONAL OBSESSIONS OF R. CRUMB

CHOICE OF ETHNIC GROUP } JEWISH, JAPANESE, HAWAIIAN, SAMOAN, SCANDINAVIAN, GERMAN, ANGLO-SAXON, IRISH, RUSSIAN, POLISH, AMERICAN MIXTURE, MEXICAN, ITALIAN, CHINESE, NEGRO

HEIGHT, UNIMPORTANT BUT PREFERABLY TALL

SKIN COLOR UNIMPORTANT HAIR UNIMPORTANT

FULL LIPS BIG TEETH

STRONG, STRAIGHT BACK STRONG NECK & SHOULDERS

FIRM BREASTS— SIZE UNIMPORTANT →

STRONG ARMS

FAIRLY SMALL IN THE WAIST

EXAGGERATED FORWARD PELVIC THRUST →

ROUND, FULL BELLY →

EXCEPTIONALLY LARGE, WELL-ENDOWED BUT FIRM BUTTOCKS WITH "SHELF" EFFECT

LARGE THIGHS

LARGE MUSCULAR LEGS IN GENERAL

THICK ANKLES

LARGE, WIDE, STRONG FEET

sketchbook page, 1975

sketchbook page, 1990

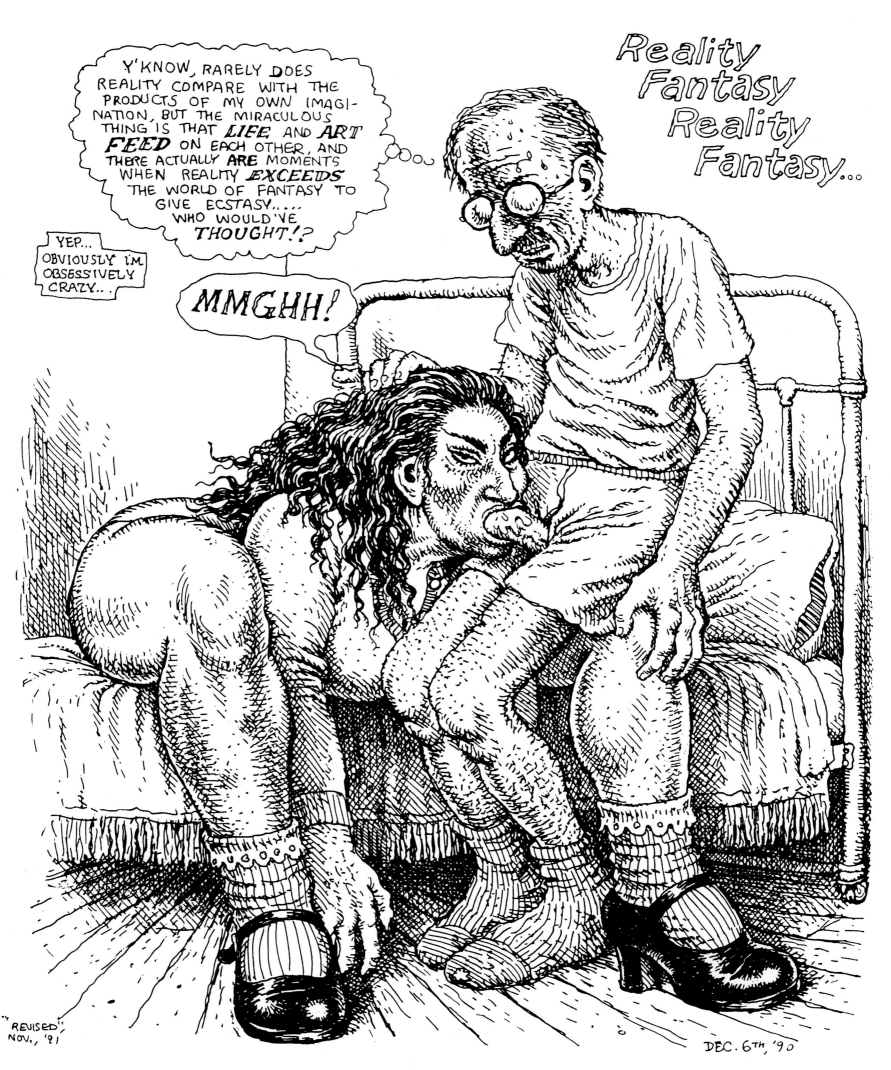

sketchbook page, 1990-91

126

Robert Crumb and Aline
Kominsky, mid-'70s

The
Profile
ALINE KOMINSKY
— JAN. '75 —

sketchbook page, 1975

Robert Crumb and Aline Kominsky,
"Let's Have a Little Talk," *Dirty
Laundry Comics* no. 1, 1974

sketchbook page, 1975

"TO BE A SINCERE, SERIOUS ARTIST IN AMERICA IS TO BE A LOSER."

— R. CRUMB

Aline's Legs
NOV., '87

# "THE SEVENTIES WAS THE 'BURNOUT DECADE!' THE BIG PARTY WAS OVER!"

IT WAS VERY CONFUSING FOR A LOT OF US. THE OLD WORK-A-DAY CAPITALIST REALITY REASSERTED ITSELF WITH GREAT FORCEFULNESS AND SWAMPED THE OPTIMISM OF THE HIPPIES. THE "MOVEMENT" GOT BOGGED DOWN AND BROKE UP INTO FACTIONS THAT WEREN'T COMFORTABLE WITH EACH OTHER; THE FEMINISTS, BLACK POWER, EASTERN RELIGION PEOPLE, JESUS FREAKS, THIS ONE, THAT ONE. A LOT OF PEOPLE SIMPLY BURNED OUT FROM TOO MUCH DOPE AND LSD. SOME OF THE WORST TENDENCIES IN AMERICA THAT THE HIPPIES WERE INITIALLY WITHDRAWING FROM CONTINUED AND EVEN PICKED UP AND BECAME WORSE, LIKE THE CORPORATIZATION OF CULTURE, THE DEVELOPMENT OF SHOPPING MALLS AND ALL THAT CRAP. THE CULTURE BECAME WORSE AND WORSE. CHARLIE MANSON CAME ALONG AND PROVED THAT THE HIPPIE THING WASN'T INFALLIBLE. HIPPIES COULD KILL. SHOCKING! WHAT A BRINGDOWN! IN 1972, NIXON WAS RE-ELECTED ... "FOUR MORE YEARS." BUMMER!

ONCE I GOT POPULAR WITH *ZAP COMIX*, A LOT OF OTHER PUBLISHERS WANTED WORK FROM ME. I REALLY TRIED TO KEEP THEM ALL HAPPY IN THE EARLY SEVENTIES, AND MY DRAWING FELL INTO A STYLISTIC RUT. I LOST INSPIRATION IN THE LINE QUALITY ITSELF. THAT WORK IS NOT VERY ATTRACTIVE TO ME WHEN I LOOK AT IT NOW. THE IDEAL THING IS TO BE INSPIRED AT THE MOMENT YOU'RE DRAWING, WHICH I HAD BEEN IN 1967, '68, '69. AFTER THAT, EVEN THOUGH I WAS STILL FULL OF IDEAS, I JUST CRANKED OUT PAGES TO GET OUT PRODUCT. I COULD DO TWO PAGES A DAY IF I WAS LEFT ALONE AND NOT PESTERED BY PEOPLE EVERY TWO SECONDS. I NEVER BOUGHT MARIJUANA BECAUSE THERE WAS ALWAYS SOMEONE PASSING ME THE FUCKING JOINT SINCE I WAS "MR. COOL-HIPPIE-CARTOONIST." IT WAS UNTHINKABLE TO SAY NO TO IT. IT TOOK ME A LONG TIME TO FIGURE OUT A PRETEXT FOR REFUSING IT BECAUSE "EVERYBODY MUST GET STONED." EVERY DAY, WITHOUT QUESTION ... LIKE EATING OR SHITTING. NO PLAN! NO REASON TO DO ANYTHING! JUST PEOPLE SITTING AROUND SMOKING DOPE WANTING TO BE ENTERTAINED. THEY THOUGHT MY CABIN IN POTTER VALLEY WAS HIP AND COOL. SO I GOT STONED AND TRIED TO AMUSE THEM BY PLAYING OLD RECORDS. SINCE I COULDN'T DRAW WITH A ROOM FULL OF PEOPLE, I'D WAIT UNTIL THEY ALL WENT TO BED, AND THEN I'D DRAW THROUGH THE NIGHT TO GET MY PAGES DONE, THEN SLEEP LATE. FINALLY I BEGAN REFUSING THE JOINT AND TELLING THEM THAT IT WAS MAKING ME PARANOID AND HANGING UP MY ABILITY TO WORK. I COULDN'T MAKE AN ARTISTIC DECISION WHEN I WAS STONED. IT STOPPED BEING FUN. I MOVED TO THE CENTRAL VALLEY, WHERE I HAD MORE TIME AND, AS SOON AS I QUIT SMOKING MARIJUANA, MY INTEREST IN DRAWING AS A DISCIPLINE CAME BACK. I BEGAN DRAWING FROM LIFE AGAIN. FOR 10 YEARS, MY WORK HAD BEEN FUELED BY PSYCHEDELIC VISIONS. YOU NEED LINEAR THINKING TO DRAW FROM LIFE. IT'S JUST WORK-A-DAY ... GET TO IT! THERE IS ALWAYS A LOW-LEVEL MUSE THAT'S THERE. YOU'RE NOT GOING TO PERSIST IF YOU'RE SITTING AROUND WAITING TO BE KNOCKED ON YOUR ASS BY A MAJOR INSPIRATION.

I BASICALLY LIVED ON WELFARE UNTIL 1972. THEN ENOUGH MONEY STARTED COMING IN THAT WE FELT WE COULD TAKE OURSELVES OFF THE WELFARE ROLL. BUT WHEN THE MONEY STARTED TO POUR IN, THAT CREATED YET ANOTHER LEVEL OF UGLY INSANITY: LAWYERS! ACCOUNTANTS! I.R.S. AGENTS! OH, IT WAS HORRIBLE! BUT MY LIFE WAS CHANGED PERMANENTLY, AND IT NEVER WENT BACK TO MY INCONSEQUENTIAL, INVISIBLE PRE-1968 PERIOD.

THINGS GOT REALLY CRAZY, AND HAVE BEEN EVER SINCE! LUCKILY, I MET ALINE, WHO HAS SAVED MY LIFE.

I REMEMBER ONCE IN 1973 BEING AT THIS DINNER WITH ALL THESE PEOPLE AND FEELING SO BURNED OUT FROM ALL THE BULLSHIT! I WAS SITTING THERE FEELING REAL SORRY FOR MYSELF, JUST SULKING WITH ALL THESE PEOPLE AROUND LAUGHING, EATING, DRINKING AND SMOKING DOPE. I FELT SWAMPED AND OVERWHELMED BY IT ALL. THEN SUDDENLY, I REALIZED THAT BEFORE I HAD FAME, I FELT SORRY FOR MYSELF BECAUSE I WAS IGNORED. EITHER WAY, YOU JUST HAVE TO DEAL WITH IT. WORK ON IT! THAT KIND OF HELPED TO RELIEVE THE SELF-PITY I WAS FEELING. I REALIZED THAT I WAS NO WORSE OFF THAN BEFORE. BETTER, ACTUALLY. AT LEAST I NOW HAD A CUTE GIRLFRIEND WITH A PHENOMENAL STEATOPYGIC ASS! IT IS AN ONGOING PROCESS I HAVE TO DEAL WITH DAY BY DAY. WHEN I'M ALONE, I FEEL LIKE I'M GETTING A GRIP ON THINGS. I CAN THINK STRAIGHT IF I HAVE EXTENDED PERIODS OF SOLITUDE. I NEED THAT TO GET WORK DONE. IT'S IMPORTANT. I COULD NEVER STAND THE BOXES THAT PEOPLE TRY TO PUT YOU IN. EVEN NOW, I'M STRUGGLING WITH THE "FAMOUS CARTOONIST" BOX. IT'S A MILLSTONE AROUND MY NECK BUT THERE ARE SOME PERKS ... I LIVE IN FRANCE, I'VE GOT CENTRAL HEATING, THE WIFE LOVES THOSE BIG CHECKS AND SO ON.

TO ESCAPE THE PRESSURES OF THE FAME BULLSHIT ATTACHED TO ME BY THE COMIC BOOK WORLD, I STARTED TO HANG OUT MORE WITH BOB ARMSTRONG AND AL DODGE AND PLAY MUSIC. I LIKED BEING PART OF A MUSIC GANG, AND I HAD MORE IN COMMON WITH THEM AS FAR AS CULTURAL INTERESTS. WE'D LISTEN TO OLD MUSIC AND TALK ABOUT WOMEN IN A WAY THAT I WAS MUCH MORE COMFORTABLE WITH. I WAS STILL GETTING ARTWORK DONE, BUT IT WASN'T THE MAIN THING. AS R. CRUMB AND HIS KEEP ON TRUCKIN' ORCHESTRA, WE CUT SOME 78s IN MAY 1972. IT WAS MY IDEA — A NOVELTY THING. WE HIT THE ROAD, ENDING UP IN ASPEN, COLORADO, SLEEPING ON THE FLOOR OF A MUSIC STORE AND FOOLING AROUND PLAYING MUSIC. LO AND BEHOLD, WE GOT A PAYING GIG PLAYING FOR THE ANNUAL BASH OF THE ASPEN SKI PATROL. WE THOUGHT WE WERE BIG TIME PROFESSIONALS, AND AL THOUGHT WE COULD TURN THIS INTO SOMETHING SINCE I WAS SOMEWHAT FAMOUS, BUT WE BOMBED TOTALLY. THOSE SKI-PATROL ALPHA MALES AND THEIR GIRL FRIENDS HATED US. WE RUINED THEIR PARTY. THEN NICK PERLS WANTED US TO DO AN ALBUM. HE WAS TOTALLY CYNICAL ABOUT THE BAND. HE NEVER SAID SO, BUT YOU COULD TELL HE THOUGHT OUR MUSIC WAS CRAP. HE FIGURED MY NAME ALONE WOULD SELL RECORDS. WE GOT TERRY ZWIGOFF TO LEARN TO PLAY THE CELLO, AND THE BAND WAS RENAMED R. CRUMB AND THE CHEAP SUIT SERENADERS. WE WERE PLAYING ON THE STREETS OF SAN FRANCISCO. FOR THOSE GUYS, EARNING $15 PLAYING ALL DAY ON THE STREET WAS BIG TIME. THE SUITS WOULD PLAY ALL THESE COFFEEHOUSES AND COMIX FANS WOULD SHOW UP TO PESTER ME. ONCE IN A WHILE, THERE WOULD BE A GIRL, BUT THE SUITS WEREN'T EXACTLY A BAND THAT DROVE GIRLS CRAZY! WE WERE PLAYING SCORNED INSTRUMENTS: BANJOS, MANDOLINS, HAWAIIAN GUITAR, ACCORDION, CELLO AND THE MUSICAL SAW. NOT EXACTLY A SEXY BUNCH OF INSTRUMENTS FOR THE LADIES!

THE SUITS YEARS LASTED FROM '72 TO '78. IN 1995, WE GOT TOGETHER FOR A EUROPEAN TOUR. I ENJOYED THAT. PLAYING MUSIC WAS NEVER THE PROBLEM, BUT THE PUBLIC EXPOSURE WAS HARD FOR ME TO DEAL WITH. BEING PESTERED BY FUCKING JOURNALISTS IS A NIGHTMARE. I'VE DEVELOPED SUCH LOATHING FOR JOURNALISTS AND MEDIA PEOPLE. I GUESS I'M UNGRATEFUL, HUH?

*opposite*, sketchbook page, 1990

Spain Rodriguez, Victor Moscoso, S. Clay Wilson, Gilbert Shelton, Rick Griffin, Robert Crumb and Robert Williams, "Mammy Jama," *Zap Comix* no. 6, 1973

*opposite page: top,* The Zap Cartoonists (*left to right,* S. Clay Wilson, Victor Moscoso, Gilbert Shelton, Rick Griffin, Spain, Robert Williams, and Robert Crumb, 1972-73)

*opposite page: bottom,* the Keep On Truckin' Orchestra on their cross-country tour, 1972 (*left to right,* Bob Armstrong, Robert Crumb and Al Dodge).

"Remember Keep on Truckin'?"
*XYZ Comics*, 1972

"What is it About People When They're Boppin' and Jivin' That's so Repugnant to Me??" sketchbook, 1990

OLDER MUSIC AND THE ANCIENT, TRADITIONAL DANCES OF ETHNIC PEOPLES DON'T HAVE THE SAME AFFECT ON ME AT ALL... THEY LIFT MY SPIRIT, AND ALMOST MAKE ME WANT TO DANCE MYSELF...

WHOOPEE!!

WHEN I WAS YOUNG AND TOOK LSD, I BECAME ACUTELY SENSITIVE TO THE RHYTHMS OF CULTURAL DEATH IN MODERN MUSIC...

BECAUSE MUSIC IS THE SOUL OF A HUMAN CULTURE...

IN MY OWN SPACED OUT, INARTICULATE WAY, I TRIED TO DRAW THE IMAGES I SAW IN MY MIND WHEN I HEARD MODERN POP MUSIC ON LSD... CLOWNISH FOOLS' BOPPIN' AND JIVIN' IN THE GARBAGE HEAP THEY WERE MAKING OUT OF THE EARTH!

1966 SKETCH BOOK

IT WAS ALL A POWERFUL REACTION TO THIS UGLY MODERN POP MUSIC!!

...MIXED WITH THIS REPULSION WAS A SENSE OF COMPASSION... IT'S NOT THEIR FAULT... THEY DON'T KNOW... THEY'RE JUST TRYING TO HAVE A GOOD TIME... THESE DRAWINGS HAD A KIND OF ALMOST HAPPY LOOK TO THEM...

WHUPPO!!

THE SUBTLE, COMPLEX CONTRADICTIONS INVOLVED IN THESE IMAGES WERE TOO MUCH FOR MY SIMPLE, UNSOPHISTICATED, SCRAMBLED YOUNG MIND... CONSEQUENTLY, I WAS *FOOLED* BY MY OWN DRAWINGS!!

HIS DOWNFALL: A GIANT *EGO!* THINKS HE'S OH SO *CLEVER*

HA HA HA!

OTHER PEOPLE THOUGHT THEY WERE HAPPY IMAGES OF RELAXED CARTOON CHARACTERS JUST HAVIN' A GOOD OL' TIME... SO *I DID TOO!* THESE DRAWINGS BECAME SYMBOLS OF THE *HANG-LOOSE* ATTITUDE OF THE LATE SIXTIES!!

I LOST MY WAY... I BECAME CONFUSED ABOUT WHAT IT WAS I WAS DOING, SAYING IN MY ART...

I FORGOT WHAT THEY REALLY WERE... *PICTOGRAPHS OF THE DANCE OF DEATH!*

YO!

*SO KEEP ON TRUCKIN', SHMUCKS!*

...PICKIN' 'EM UP AN' LAYIN' 'EM DOWN... →

KA-BOOM KA-BOOM KA-BOOM

HUP HUP!

DON'T FORGET, BOB, THAT IT WAS THE *COMPASSION*, THE *LOVING* FORGIVENESS IN THE FACE OF THIS TERRIBLE KNOWLEDGE THAT THEY FOUND SO APPEALING IN YOUR CARTOONS, THAT MADE YOU SO POPULAR, THAT GOT YOU LAID, THAT EARNED YOU A LIVING... KEEP IT IN MIND!!

143

144

"Crybaby Beanhead in Crybaby's Blues," *Arcade* no. 5, 1976

145

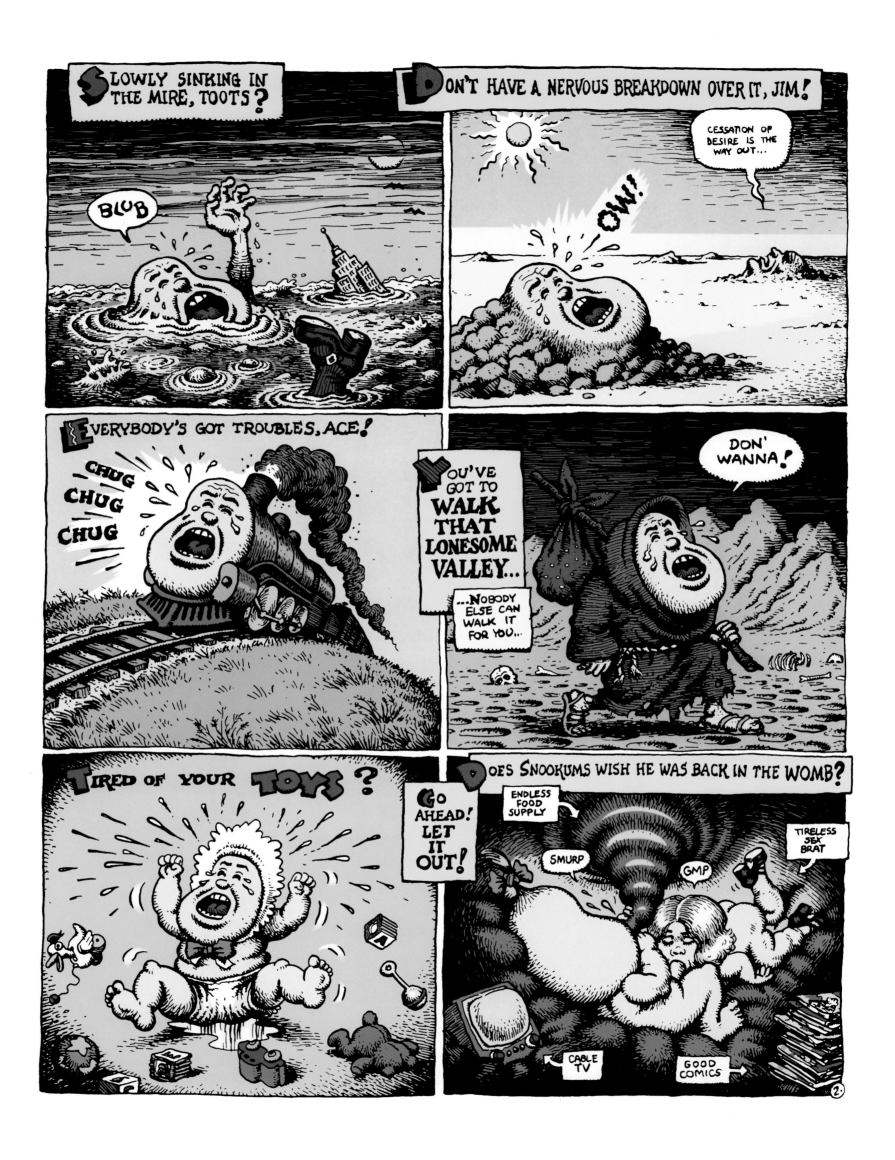

146

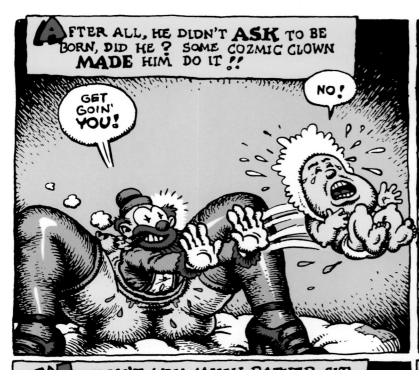

AFTER ALL, HE DIDN'T **ASK** TO BE BORN, DID HE? SOME COZMIC CLOWN **MADE** HIM DO IT!!

GET GOIN' YOU!

NO!

**IS** IT TOO HARD TO GET OUT THERE AND **FACE LIFE**?!

WOULDN'T YOU MUCH RATHER SIT BACK AND ENJOY IT ALL FROM A DISTANCE??

HM... HOW INTERESTING...

HA HA HA

SCORE CARD

**BUT** NO... INSTEAD HE'S DRAGGED DOWN EVER DEEPER INTO THE MESS BY HIS **WANTS**!

MUNCH... ARE WE ALMOST THERE YET?

LEGGO, DOC! I'LL SAVE Y'!

SHANGRILA OR BUST

HE WANTS! HE WANTS! HE'S A REGULAR "I WANT" BOY!

I WANNIT! I WANNIT! I WANNIT! I WANNIT! I WANNIT!

HE WANTS THINGS! NOT GREAT THINGS, BUT CHEAP, MUNDANE EVERYDAY THINGS.!!

GIMME! GIMME! GIMME DIS! GIMME DAT!

HE WANTS A PIECE OF **FRENCH TOAST**!

148

"Frosty the Snowman
and His Friends,"
*Arcade* no. 4, 1975

150

151

153

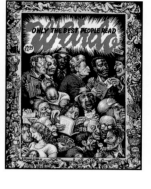

"I Remember the Sixties,"
*Weirdo* no. 4, 1981

IT WAS HIP TO DESPISE ALL "PIGS" (COPS) AS A MATTER OF COURSE.

HOW TIMES HAVE CHANGED! NOW I'M RELIEVED TO SEE A COP CAR WHEN I'M WALKIN' DOWN CITY STREETS!

BUT BACK THEN WE WANTED TO BREAK DOWN ALL "LAW'N'ORDER". WE HATED ALL SYMBOLS OF AUTHORITY. ANYTHING ASSOCIATED WITH OUR PARENTS AND THEIR VALUES WAS POISON TO US, AND WE EXPRESSED OURSELVES!

THE REBELLION OF THE "YOUTH CULTURE" WAS VERY SELF-CONSCIOUS AND STYLISTIC...

A LOT OF THESE MIDDLE-CLASS "DROP-OUTS" BEGAN LIVING IN THEIR OWN LSD-INSPIRED FAIRY-TALE LAND, LIKE THE GIRL ON HAIGHT STREET WHO WAS KNOWN ONLY AS "GINGERBREAD PRINCESS."

BUT IT COULDN'T LAST... THEY WERE LIKE HELPLESS LITTLE LAMBS AND THE HUNGRY WOLVES WERE MOVING IN...

THE LIGHT-HEARTED DAYS OF THE "FLOWER-CHILDREN" BEGAN TO WAIN AFTER THE "SUMMER OF LOVE"... THE LOW-LIFES AND THE GREEDY WERE SPREADING "BAD VIBES." THE SCENE WAS GETTING TOO "HEAVY" FOR A LOT OF PEOPLE... GANGS OF OUTLAW BIKERS WERE TAKING OVER HAIGHT STREET....

A SCRUFFIER BREED OF HIPPIES BEGAN TO APPEAR.... THEIR BRAND OF HIPNESS WAS OFFENSIVE TO THE REFINED SENSIBILITIES OF THOSE FROM MORE UPPER CLASS ORIGINS.

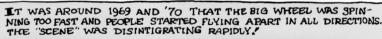

BY 1969 A DEMON CALLED PARANOIA STALKED THE HAIGHT... THE DRUGS GOT HARDER AND PEOPLE WERE CARRYING GUNS... RIP-OFFS, MURDERS, RAPE, COMMERCIALIZATION AND OTHER PLAGUES DESCENDED ON THE NEIGHBORHOOD.... IT WAS A GRIM FUCKIN' SPECTACLE...

IT WAS AROUND 1969 AND '70 THAT THE BIG WHEEL WAS SPINNING TOO FAST AND PEOPLE STARTED FLYING APART IN ALL DIRECTIONS. THE "SCENE" WAS DISINTIGRATING RAPIDLY!

IT WASN'T SO OBVIOUS THEN THAT WE WERE RIDING ON THE CREST OF A WAVE... WE THOUGHT WE'D NEVER COME DOWN!!

BUT THE WAVE FINALLY CRASHED ON THE BEACH.....

LEAVING ALOT OF PEOPLE LAYING THERE ALL LIMP AND SOGGY WITH A MOUTHFUL OF SALT WATER.

FOR ABOUT A YEAR THERE I OFTEN EXPERIENCED A STRANGE DIZZY SENSATION AS IF THE VERY EARTH ITSELF WAS RAPIDLY FALLING THROUGH SPACE!! ...IT WAS A HIGH-SPEED ELEVATOR GOING DOWN, DOWN, DOWN...

I WAS A "BURN-OUT" CASE FOR YEARS. ...ALL THE LSD...ALL THE DOPE... THE CRAZINESS...MY MIND WAS SHOT.

I'M NOT SO SURE I EVER TOTALLY RECOVERED, BUT HELL, I'M DOIN' BETTER THAN SOME OTHER SIXTIES CASUALTIES... SOME OF 'EM ARE STILL OUT THERE ON HAIGHT STREET... STILL DOING ALL THE DRUGS, STILL LIVING IN "CRASH-PADS", ETC.

SOME OF THEM BECAME HOPELESS RELIGIOUS FANATICS OF ONE "CULT" OR ANOTHER...EVERY ONE A "SPACE CASE"...

OTHERS DECIDED TO CUT OUT ALL THIS CHILDISH NONSENSE, DROPPED BACK IN AND KNUCKLED DOWN... YOU SEE THEM NOW CLAWING THEIR WAY TO THE TOP, MAKING BUCKS HAND OVER FIST, BUYING HOT TUBS...

STILL OTHERS SCATTERED TO THE HILLS IN A "BACK-TO-THE-LAND" MOVEMENT, PRESERVING INTACT THE TRAPPINGS OF THE HIPPY SUBCULTURE THEY TOOK WITH THEM. IT'S NOT A BAD LIFE FOR A LOT OF THESE "HIPPY-BILLIES."

YEAH, BUT WHO CARES ABOUT THE SIXTIES ANYMORE, ANYWAY? IT'S ALL ANCIENT HISTORY BY NOW.. THIS IS 1982, AND IT'S A WHOLE NEW BALL-GAME... THE YOUTH TODAY IS COMING OUT OF A DIFFERENT BAG, DEFINITELY!

AH, BUT THOSE CRAZY, LAZY, HAZY DAYS OF 1965, '66, '67...THOSE UNFORGETTABLE LSD TRIPS.... (SOMETIMES I WISH I COULD FORGET THEM) ...LET ME TELL YOU ABOUT SOME OF MY LSD TRIPS...

LIKE THE TIME I WAS CERTAIN THAT I WAS, IN FACT, JESUS CHRIST ON THE CROSS, SUFFERING FOR THE SINS OF ALL HUMANITY (CATHOLIC UPBRINGING) ...WOW, THAT WAS POWERFUL ACID!!

"It's a Miracle," sketchbook page, 1976

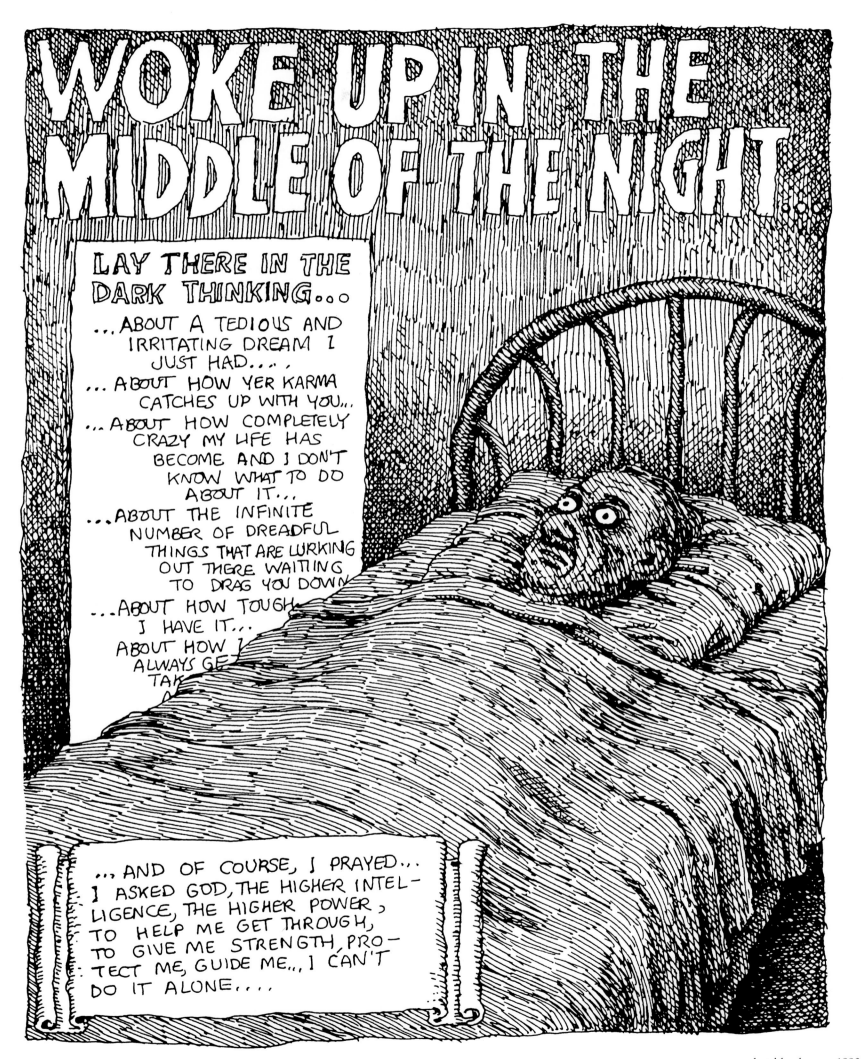

WOKE UP IN THE MIDDLE OF THE NIGHT

LAY THERE IN THE DARK THINKING...

...ABOUT A TEDIOUS AND IRRITATING DREAM I JUST HAD....

...ABOUT HOW YER KARMA CATCHES UP WITH YOU...

...ABOUT HOW COMPLETELY CRAZY MY LIFE HAS BECOME AND I DON'T KNOW WHAT TO DO ABOUT IT...

...ABOUT THE INFINITE NUMBER OF DREADFUL THINGS THAT ARE LURKING OUT THERE WAITING TO DRAG YOU DOWN

...ABOUT HOW TOUGH I HAVE IT...

ABOUT HOW I ALWAYS GET TAK...

...AND OF COURSE, I PRAYED... I ASKED GOD, THE HIGHER INTELLIGENCE, THE HIGHER POWER, TO HELP ME GET THROUGH, TO GIVE ME STRENGTH, PROTECT ME, GUIDE ME.., I CAN'T DO IT ALONE....

sketchbook page, 1990

sketchbook page, early '90s

THE LITTLE GUY
THAT LIVES IN-
SIDE MY BRAIN

JAN. 30TH '86

163

AN
EXPRESSION
I MAKE
ALOT

('CAUSE MY GLASSES
ARE ALWAYS
SLIDING DOWN... )

OCT. 30TH
1983

sketchbook page, 1983

166

"What's wrong with Me" Dept:

# No Rest for the Wicked

IN THE MORNING: I AWAKE FROM "THE SLEEP WHICH DOES NOT REFRESH..."

OH GOD

MY MIND IS ALWAYS BUSY TRYING TO SORT OUT THE BYZANTINE ENTANGLEMENTS OF MY OVERLY COMPLEX LIFE...

HOW DID THINGS EVER GET TO THIS POINT ?!?

AS MARK TWAIN ONCE SAID ABOUT AMERICA: "IT IS A CIVILIZATION WHICH HAS DESTROYED THE SIMPLICITY AND REPOSE OF LIFE; REPLACED IT'S CONTENTMENT, IT'S POETRY, IT'S SOFT ROMANTIC DREAMS AND VISIONS WITH THE MONEY FEVER, SORDID IDEALS, VULGAR AMBITIONS, AND THE SLEEP WHICH DOES NOT REFRESH..."

MONEY IS THE ROOT OF ALL EVIL! "THE LACK OF MONEY IS THE ROOT OF ALL EVIL." —MARK TWAIN

THAT'S ME ALRIGHT!!

WHAT AM I GONNA DO?!

I'VE BEEN GETTING A LOT OF HEAD-ACHES LATELY...

AM I BECOMING ADDICTED TO THE FOLDING GREEN STUFF? I SEEM TO NEED MORE AND MORE OF IT...

CAN'T LIVE WITH IT AND CAN'T LIVE WITHOUT IT

GODDAMN THIS INFLATION!!

BUT SOMETIMES WHEN I THINK ABOUT IT, I CAN'T BELIEVE HOW LUCKY I AM! I'M A WHITE AMERICAN MALE, I'M TALENTED, SUCCESSFUL, LOVED BY WOMEN, RESPECTED BY MY PEERS, I HAVE A FINE INTELLIGENT SON... I.....

OH GOD... MY SON..

SO OLD BEFORE HIS TIME

I LOVE THAT BOY... HE'S SUCH A CRAZY LITTLE FELLA... I'M NO GOOD AS A FATHER... I'VE SHIRKED MY PARENTAL DUTIES.. I SHOULD GO SEE HIM MORE OFTEN.. HE NEEDS ME... OH DEAR LORD, WHAT AM I GONNA DO ??

HOW AM I GONNA END THIS CHAOS, THIS COMPLICATED MESS THAT MY LIFE HAS BECOME... TOO MANY RESPONSIBILITIES, TOO MANY COMMITMENTS... I'VE GOT TO TRIM IT DOWN SOMEHOW.... GOT TO GET CONTROL OF MYSELF SOMEHOW.. GOT TO..".

RUN, BOB, RUN!

"GIVE ME THE SIMPLE LIFE!"

sketchbook page, 1975

sketchbook page, 1980s

sketchbook page, 1994

sketchbook page, 1980s

"Mr. Sicko's Diary," sketchbook page, 1982

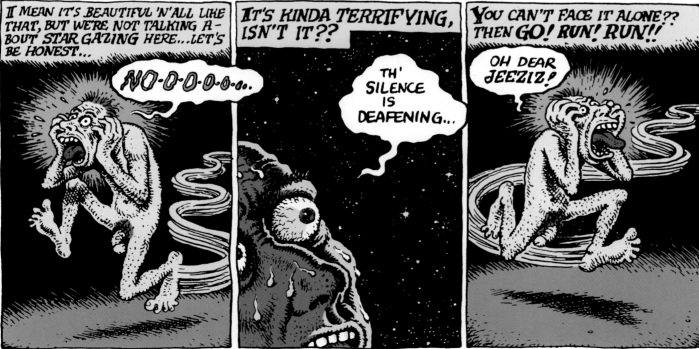

"Can You Stand Alone and Face Up to the Universe?" *Hup* no. 4, 1992

RUN TO YOUR JESUS! THROW YOURSELF AT THE FOOT OF THE CROSS!!

WHINE TO YOUR KRISHNA! YOUR BUDDHA! YOUR MOHAMMED!

..OR, IF THAT AIN'T TO YOUR LIKIN', GET FUCKED UP! NUMB THE SENSES!

YEAH, TRUE... SOONER OR LATER YOU'RE GONNA WAKE UP SOBER... ALONE...IN THE DARK...BUT THEN, DON'T WE ALL...

BUMMER...

A COUPLE A GOOD-NATURED SLOBS... WHAT'D THEY KNOW??

174

I GUESS TH' POINT IS, MAYBE IT'S NOT NECESSARY TO "DENY THE FLESH" IN ORDER TO BE "SPIRITUAL"... I HOPE NOT! A GREAT REVELATION WAS GIVEN RECENTLY TO A WHITE ANTHROPOLOGIST BY A PIGMY CHIEFTAIN. HE SAID...

LIFE IS MEANT TO BE ENJOYED.

REPORTED IN "NATIONAL GEOGRAPHIC" MAGAZINE

STILL, IT'S EVERY HUMAN BEING'S PERSONAL RESPONSIBILITY TO BECOME AS ENLIGHTENED AS POSSIBLE.... NO ONE'S EXCUSED ON GROUNDS OF IGNORANCE, POVERTY, OR OPPRESSION...

ENLIGHTEN:
1. To give intellectual or spiritual light to; instruct, impart knowledge to.
— AMERICAN COLLEGE DICTIONARY

LIKE IT OR NOT OUR MINDS ARE — INTERESTED — FASCINATED — ATTRACTED TO — ETERNITY — INFINITY — WE'RE ANIMALS BUT WE'RE ALSO SOMETHING MORE...

? ?

I LIKE TA THINK SO... I WONDER WHAT THAT COULD BE...

OH WELL, I'LL PONDER IT LATER... AFTER I'VE RAVAGED THIS FINE FEMALE...

OH YOU CYNICS! YOU INTELLECTUALS, WITH YOUR COLLEGE EDUCATIONS! I CAN JUST HEAR YOU...

SIGH! AH YES! TH' WONDER OF IT ALL! HO HUM!

TA HA HA... SUCH MUDDLE-HEADED NONSENSE!

IT'S HIS HEAVY CATHOLIC UPBRINGING COMING OUT...

NOTHING ABOUT TEN YEARS ON TH' COUCH WOULDN'T CURE!

HA HA HA

OKAY, SO I'M A LITTLE SOPHOMORIC, BUT, HEY, I DON'T "BELIEVE IN GOD" EITHER...

BUT COME ON, ADMIT IT... EVEN YOU FEEL FINALLY, TERRIBLY... ALONE... WELL, MAYBE YOU DON'T... MAYBE YOU'RE SO DAMN TOUGH-MINDED, YOU'RE NOT BOTHERED BY SUCH FEELINGS...

MAYBE YOU'RE RIGHT... IT'S ALL JUST CHEMICALS IN THE BRAIN 'N' THINGS LIKE THAT...

MAYBE I'M JUST WEAK... I CAN'T TAKE IT... I WANT A BIG MOMMY TO TAKE CARE OF ME... AN OMNIPOTENT SOURCE OF SOLACE AND COMFORT.

EVVATHANG GONE BE JES' FINE NOW, HONEY CHILE..

MMM... SING ME A GOSPEL HYMN, MAMMY!

HIDE ME OVER IN TH' ROCK OF AGES, CLEFT FOR ME, CLEFT FOR ME...

MAN, THESE BIG TITTIES ARE FIRM!

THIS IS EMBARRASSING TO ADMIT, BUT THERE ARE TIMES, DESPERATE MOMENTS, WHEN I FEEL SO LOST, SO VEXED AND HELPLESS, THAT I PRAY... IT'S TRUE... I APPEAL... I ENTREAT SOME "HIGHER POWER" IN THE UNIVERSE...

HELP ME! HELP ME TO BE STRONG! RESOLUTE!! AN'— AN'—LIKE THAT...

175

ORGANIZED CHURCHES LIKE CHRISTIANITY HAVE GIVEN THE *SPIRITUAL* SUCH A BAD NAME, IT MAKES ME FEEL LIKE A DANG *FOOL* TA EVEN BE UP HERE *TALKING* ABOUT SUCH THINGS!

PREACHER BOB

AH, HE'S JUST GETTING *WARMED UP!*

A HEALTHY *SKEPTICISM* IS TO BE ENCOURAGED... I WOULDN'T ADVISE ACCEPTING *ANYTHING* ON *FAITH!* EVERYTHING'S OPEN TO *QUESTION!* CUTTING THROUGH THE LAYERS OF *JIVE BULLSHIT* IS HALF THE BATTLE!

MAYBE THE *SKEPTIC* IN ME WOULD SAY THIS *"HIGHER INTELLIGENCE"* IS JUST THE VAST UNUSED POTENTIAL INSIDE THE *HUMAN BRAIN!*

HM...

TAP TAP

The Human Brain
OR POSSIBLY A CAULIFLOWER

I'M SURE IT IS, BUT IT'S MORE THAN THAT... *BIGGER* THAN THAT! AS WE ALL KNOW, THERE EXISTS *BILLIONS* OF STARS IN THE UNIVERSE... *DIMENSIONS* UNKNOWN TO US... TH' PLACE IS *INFINITE!*

IT *BOGGLES* TH' MIND!

OOH-WEE!

YEAH MAN!

YOU MEAN T' TELL ME, SOMEWHERE IN ALL THAT, THERE *ISN'T* ANOTHER INTELLIGENT LIFE FORM?? AND ONE MORE ADVANCED THAN US? MAYBE JUST A FEW MILLION YEARS AHEAD OF US? A FEW *BILLION??*

YOU TELL IT'!

YEAH!

SEEMS LIKE A PERFECTLY REASONABLE PROPOSITION TO ME... IT'S NOT A CRACK-POT NOTION, IS IT? AND FROM THERE, Y'SEE, YOU CAN CONTEMPLATE ALL *KINDS* OF POSSIBILITIES *!!*

PRAISE GAWD!

AY-MEN!

*"SO WHAT?"* YOU SAY... WELL, CONNECTING WITH THIS HIGHER INTELLIGENCE... THAT INTERESTS ME... NOT TO A FANATIC DEGREE OR ANYTHING... I HAVE TO DO IT MY OWN WAY... BUT, Y'KNOW... I MEAN, *SEX* IS STILL MY MAIN AREA OF STUDY, BUT... UHH...

OHH LAWD!

ME TOO, BOB!

THEY DON'T MISS IT, BROTHER!

I THINK IT CAN EVEN BE *USEFUL* IN CERTAIN WAYS... *HELPFUL* IN FINDING SOLUTIONS TO PROBLEMS.... PROBLEMS OF HEALTH, FAMILY...

MONEY...

SEX EVEN...

MAYBE...

OH YES!

MM-HM!

NOT TO MENTION THE DEEPER *EXISTENTIAL TERROR* THING... THE *VOID*... THAT, TOO, IS AN *ILLUSION*... I KNOW 'CAUSE *GOD* TOLD ME SO...

JUST NOW, IN FACT!

DIDN'T CHA HEAR 'IM?

AMEN

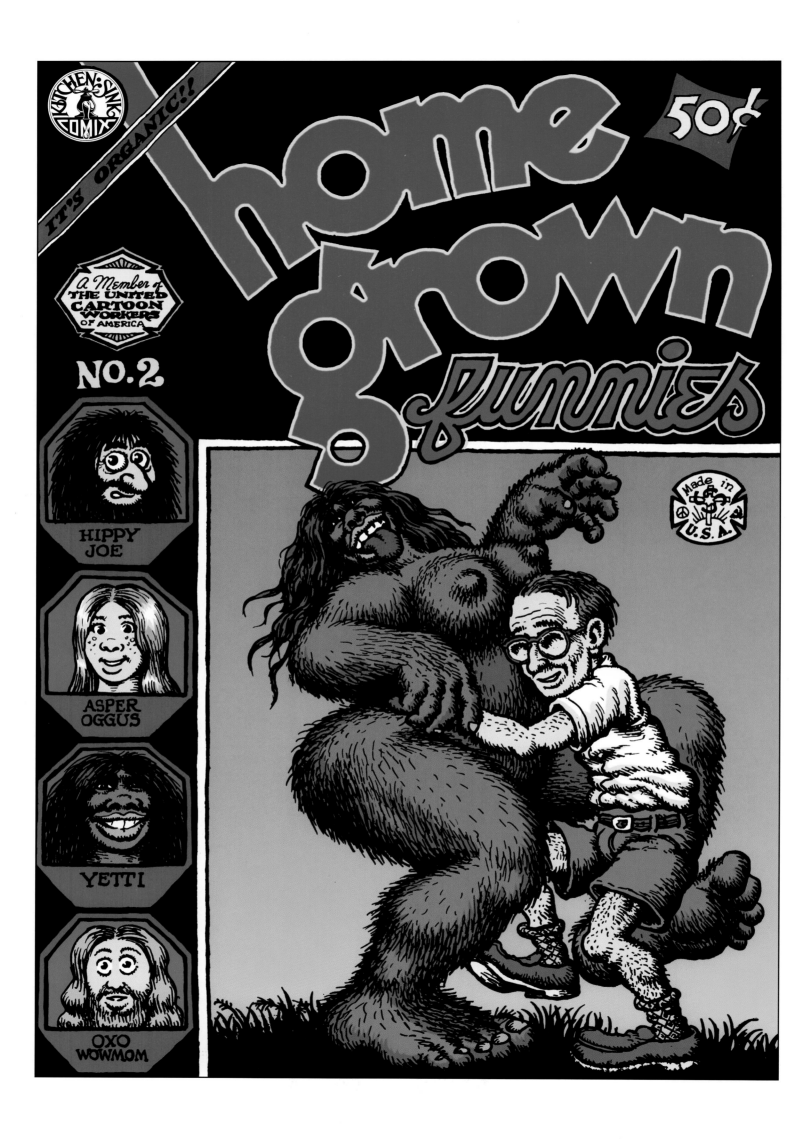

# "I BELIEVE IN EVERYTHING... UFOs, BIGFOOT, CHANNELING, ESP... I BELIEVE IT ALL!"

**D**EMONS, ANGELS, HEAVEN, HELL?...I KNOW THERE IS A HELL BECAUSE WE'RE LIVING IN IT! REINCARNATION? WHY NOT? ANYTHING YOU CAN IMAGINE PROBABLY EXISTS! HIGHER BEINGS, LOWER BEINGS, OTHER DIMENSIONS! GHOSTS! I BELIEVE ALL THAT STUFF ON *SIGHTINGS*. MAYBE I'M JUST SUGGESTIBLE, GULLIBLE...I ALSO BELIEVE THERE IS A LOT OF CHARLATANISM GOING ON IN THE WORLD, SO YOU HAVE TO BE CAREFUL, RESERVE JUDGMENT, BE SKEPTICAL BUT REMAIN OPEN. BESIDES, IT'S FUN AND EXCITING TO SPECULATE ON THESE MYSTERIES. I THINK IT IS ALL NEUROLOGICAL. SOME PEOPLE ARE JUST HARD-NOSED AND HAVE PRACTICAL MINDS, AND IT IS GOOD THAT THERE ARE PEOPLE LIKE THAT. IMAGINE IF EVERYONE IN THE WORLD WAS A NUTCASE LIKE ME.

I'VE ALWAYS HAD A CURIOSITY ABOUT THINGS LIKE BIGFOOT AND UFOs AND PARANORMAL PHENOMENA. IF YOU ACTUALLY START STUDYING THESE THINGS, THE MYSTERY AROUND THEM JUST DEEPENS AND DEEPENS. SOMETHING IS GOING ON, WHAT IS IT? WHO KNOWS? BUT ORDINARY PEOPLE HAVE SEEN THESE SASQUATCH CREATURES IN THE NORTHWEST. CAMPERS IN LAND ROVERS, FOREST RANGERS ...THEY'VE SEEN SOMETHING THAT IS OUTSIDE THE PARAMETERS THAT CIVILIZATION ASSUMES IT KNOWS. THAT'S EXCITING AND INTERESTING TO ME. LIKE UFOs AND ALIENS. I BEGAN READING ABOUT THAT STUFF WHEN A GUY I KNEW CLAIMED TO HAVE BEEN ABDUCTED AND WAS TRYING TO FIGURE IT OUT FOR HIMSELF WHAT HAD HAPPENED TO HIM. HE SENT ME SOME BOOKS TO READ, AND I'VE BEEN STUDYING THIS PHENOMENON EVER SINCE. THERE ARE SO MANY STRANGE STORIES. BUT, SEE, TO A PERSON OF PRACTICAL TEMPERAMENT LIKE A-LINE, IT'S JUST A BIG WASTE OF TIME.

**T**WENTY YEARS AGO, BOB ARMSTRONG, AL DODGE AND MYSELF WERE VISITING WARD KIMBALL. KIMBALL WAS ONE OF THE "NINE OLD MEN" WHO WORKED FOR DECADES FOR THE WALT DISNEY STUDIO. HE WAS A BIG-WIG OVER THERE. HE HAD A WONDROUS TOY COL-LECTION, LOVED OLD STEAM TRAINS AND PLAYED OLD-TIME JAZZ. HE TOLD US AN INTERESTING STORY. BACK IN THE 1950s, THEY WERE WORKING ON A SERIES ABOUT ROCKETS AND OUTER SPACE TECHNOLOGY FOR THE DISNEYLAND TV SHOW. I REMEMBER SEEING THOSE SHOWS WHEN I WAS A KID. THERE WAS A SCIENTIST NAMED WILKINS WHO WORKED ON THE PROJECT. WILKINS STARTED BRINGING AROUND THIS GUY CALLED "HUUNRATH," SUPPOSEDLY A COLLEAGUE OF HIS. KIMBALL SAID AT FIRST NO ONE TOOK MUCH NOTICE OF THE GUY HUUNRATH. HE WAS JUST KIND OF UNOBTRUSIVE.

LATER, PEOPLE STARTED ASKING, "WELL, JUST WHO IS THIS HUUNRATH?" HE WAS KIND OF STRANGE. HE DIDN'T SAY MUCH. HE WALKED KIND OF STIFFLY AND HE WORE A SUIT AND A TIE THAT WERE ILL-FITTING. THEN WILKINS AND HUUNRATH DISAPPEARED AND PEOPLE TRIED TO REMEMBER WHAT THEY COULD ABOUT HUUNRATH. WARD RECALLED THAT ONCE AT A DINNER PARTY AT HIS HOUSE, OATMEAL COOKIES WERE SERVED FOR DESSERT. HUUNRATH PICKED UP AN OATMEAL COOKIE AND WAS TURNING IT OVER IN HIS HANDS AND STUDYING IT VERY CLOSELY. THEN HE BIT OFF A LITTLE PIECE, CHEWED ON IT AWHILE AND ASKED WARD'S WIFE WHAT THE COOKIE WAS MADE OF. THE LAST TIME ANYBODY SAW WILKINS, HE SAID HE AND HUUNRATH WERE GOING "WHERE THERE WAS NO DEATH OR TAXES." THEN HE LAUGHED! WARD KIMBALL WAS VERY SERIOUS WHEN HE TOLD US THIS STORY. HE WAS AMUSED, YET HE THOUGHT IT WAS STRANGE.

I'D BE VERY CURIOUS TO GO ABOARD ONE A' THEM FLYING SAUCERS! PEOPLE WHO CLAIM THAT THIS HAS HAPPENED TO THEM ARE USUALLY COMPLETELY TERRIFIED. HARDLY ANYONE REMAINS CALM IN THAT SITUATION ... IT'S TOO EXCEEDINGLY STRANGE, BUT WHAT *IS* REALLY HAPPENING? IF YOU STUDY THE MIRACLES OF THE CATHOLIC CHURCH GOING BACK TO THE MIDDLE AGES, YOU GET THE SAME KIND OF STRANGENESS. WHAT IS IT ALL ABOUT?

*opposite*, unpublished cover, 1972; *above*, excerpt from a sketchbook page, 1975

183

184

186

189

# "TO BE INTERESTED IN OLD MUSIC IS TO BE A SOCIAL OUTCAST!"

YOU PLAY OLD RECORDS FOR MOST PEOPLE, AND, IF THEY LISTEN AT ALL, AFTER THE RECORD'S OVER THEY TURN TO YOU AND SAY, "SO WHAT IS IT YOU LIKE ABOUT THAT OLD MUSIC?" YOU JUST WANT TO THROW UP YOUR HANDS.

I BECAME CURIOUS ABOUT OLD RECORDS WHEN I WAS OUT LOOKING FOR OLD COMICS, OLD BOOKS AND STUFF LIKE THAT. I ALWAYS LIKED THE MUSIC IN OLD MOVIES, BUT I HAD NO IDEA THAT YOU COULD FIND IT ON RECORDS. BUT THEN I BEGAN TO NOTICE THAT THERE WERE THESE 78 RECORDS SITTING IN DUSTY PILES IN SECOND-HAND STORES WHEN I WAS 15 AND 16. I HAD VERY LITTLE MONEY TO SPEND, BUT I ANTED UP TEN CENTS OR A QUARTER AND BOUGHT A FEW. SOME WERE DISAPPOINTINGLY STODGY, SOME WERE OPERATIC OR DULL SALON ORCHESTRAS... THEN I PLAYED THIS ONE RECORD, AND IT THRILLED ME TO THE CORE OF MY BEING! "THAT'S IT! THAT'S THE MUSIC I'VE BEEN LOOKING FOR ALL MY LIFE!" IT WAS ANOTHER REVELATION! IT WAS A 1928 DANCE ORCHESTRA FROM ATLANTIC CITY CALLED CHARLIE FRY'S MILLION DOLLAR PIER ORCHESTRA. THE TUNE WAS "HAPPY DAYS AND LONELY NIGHTS!" TO ME... IT WAS PERFECT MUSIC! I STILL HAVE THAT RECORD, STILL PLAY IT, STILL ENJOY IT. IT HOOKED ME! FROM THEN ON I STARTED LOOKING FOR THAT KIND OF DANCE MUSIC OF THE TWENTIES. LATER, I REALIZED THAT I HAD BEEN SUFFERING FROM WHAT I CALL "SYNCOPATION DEPRIVATION" UNTIL I FOUND THIS MUSIC.

MY MUSICAL TASTES GRADUALLY SPREAD OUT FROM TWENTIES DANCE MUSIC TO BLUES, THEN TO AMERICAN WHITE COUNTRY MUSIC, THEN IRISH MUSIC, OLD MEXICAN MUSIC AND NOW, OLD-TIME FRENCH MUSIC. EVERY DAMN THING YOU CAN THINK OF FROM THAT LATE TWENTIES PERIOD, KIND OF FOCUSED AROUND THE YEAR 1930, BUILDING THROUGH THE TWENTIES AND THEN DECLINING IN THE THIRTIES. THAT WAS A GOLDEN AGE OF MUSIC! WHY 1930? THE REASONS WERE COMPLEX AND ESOTERIC. THERE WAS A LOT OF WORK STILL FOR ALL KINDS OF MUSICIANS, DANCING WAS VERY POPULAR, WELL-MADE MASS-PRODUCED INSTRUMENTS WERE CHEAP AND PLENTIFUL, ELECTRONIC MASS MEDIA HADN'T YET REPLACED LIVE MUSIC, THERE WAS STILL A LIVING RURAL CULTURE WITH ITS RICH REGIONAL DIVERSITY. IN THE UNITED STATES IN THE 1920S, IN ANY TOWN OF, SAY, 50,000 PEOPLE OR MORE, THERE WERE HUNDREDS OF PLACES THAT PROVIDED LIVE MUSIC: DANCE HALLS, HOTEL BALLROOMS, RESTAURANTS, THEATERS, NEIGHBORHOOD AND ETHNIC SOCIETIES AND CLUBS, COMPANY PICNICS, RIVER CRUISES, AMUSEMENT PARKS AND OUTDOOR PAVILIONS IN SUMMERTIME, COLLEGE AND HIGH SCHOOL AUDITORIUMS, NOT TO MENTION CHURCH MUSIC AND PEOPLE JUST PLAYING AT HOME WITH FAMILY AND FRIENDS FOR THEIR OWN AMUSEMENT. THIS FERTILE MUSICAL CLIMATE IS REFLECTED IN THE OLD 78 RECORDS OF THE PERIOD.

AN ADDED BONUS TO THE GREAT MUSIC IS THE WONDERFUL ART IN THE FORM OF LABELS, RECORD JACKETS AND ADVERTISEMENTS WHICH I COLLECT AND USE IN MY WORK. THE PEOPLE WHO DID SUCH WORK WERE JUST PEDESTRIAN COMMERCIAL ARTISTS OF THE PERIOD, BUT IT JUST HAPPENED TO BE A GOLDEN AGE OF COMMERCIAL ART SO THEY HAD ACCESS TO DESIGN MOTIFS AND THE SCHOOLING IT TOOK TO LEARN THOSE BEAUTIFUL LETTERING STYLES. IT WAS PART OF THE CULTURE SO THAT EVEN THE MOST COMMONPLACE ITEM, A CAN OF BED BUG DESTROYER, BECOMES A BEAUTIFUL OBJECT. WHEN I FIRST SAW SOME OF THIS STUFF... OLD RACE RECORD JACKETS WITH THE ORIGINAL RECORD INSIDE FRAMED ON THE WALL IN THE HOMES OF RECORD COLLECTORS I WOULD VISIT, HOW I ENVIED AND COVETED THIS STUFF! TO ME THESE THINGS WERE AS BEAUTIFUL AS THE FRESCOES IN THE SISTINE CHAPEL. THERE IS SOMETHING SWEET AND HOMESPUN ABOUT ALL THIS LOW POPULAR CULTURE STUFF OF THE TWENTIES AND WHEN I GO TO MY PARAMOUNT RECORD INDEX TO LOOK AT ADS WITH SOME TYPEFACE FROM 1928 I CAN USE IN SOME ARTWORK I'M DOING, I KNOW I'M STEALING FROM THE BEST.

YOU DON'T TOUCH THE GROOVES WHEN HANDLING RECORDS!

*opposite,* poster for film documentary *Louie Bluie,* detail, 1985; *above,* framed Vocalian race record sleeve in Crumb's studio; *right,* sketchbook detail, 1980s

191

An Obsessive Pre-occupation...a Fascination, Nay, an Intense **LOVE** for certain things of the past:

# Deep Nostalgia

In my case, particularly for America of the 1860s to 1930 period, or/and pre-industrial europe....

from the *Paramount Banjo Catalogue* c. 1926

Floyd Campbell with Vincent Lopez Combination New York

"Shorty" Cook Murray's Venetian Orchestra Los Angeles, Cal.

## Why I'm Neurotic About My Record Collection — by R. Crumb

On the one hand I love my records so much!!

"The Bumps" by Jeannette's Synco-Jazzers!! This is such a great record!! Love it love it!

SMOOCH!

On the other hand, I worry endlessly about being so attached to mere material objects...

As long as those records are in here I'll never attain higher consciousness!!

It's a sickness, really! And let's be honest, it's more than just a love of music...it's collecting mania...the thrill of possession! The owning of a fetish! The mysterious attraction of the series syndrome!!!

Oboy! I got all three of the Big Chief Henry's Indian String-Band records!!

You don't say...

Bored wife

So what! A guy's entitled to have a hobby, you might say... but where does "hobby" leave off and anal obsession take over??

Goddammit, why wont he trade me that copy of "Banjo Sam" by Wilmer Watts?!? He knows how bad I need that record... that lousy asshole!!

Ignoring music

Sometimes I think the wisest thing would be to just get rid of the whole damn collection, but then if I start thinking about that too much, I get very sad...

Oohh nooo! How could I ever part with my copy of "Happy Days and Lonely Nights" by Charlie Fry and his Million-Dollar Pier Orch.!!

Sob

I know if I did get rid of them I'd feel 2000 pounds lighter!!

I'm free! I'm free..!

Anal retentives have trouble "letting go" of things...

Let's face it, this is neurotic behavior!!

*opposite, sketchbook details, mid-'70s; this page, clockwise from the left,* Paramount race record ads from 1927-28; advertisement by Crumb for Yazoo Records, 1978

193

"That's Life," *Arcade* no. 3, 1975

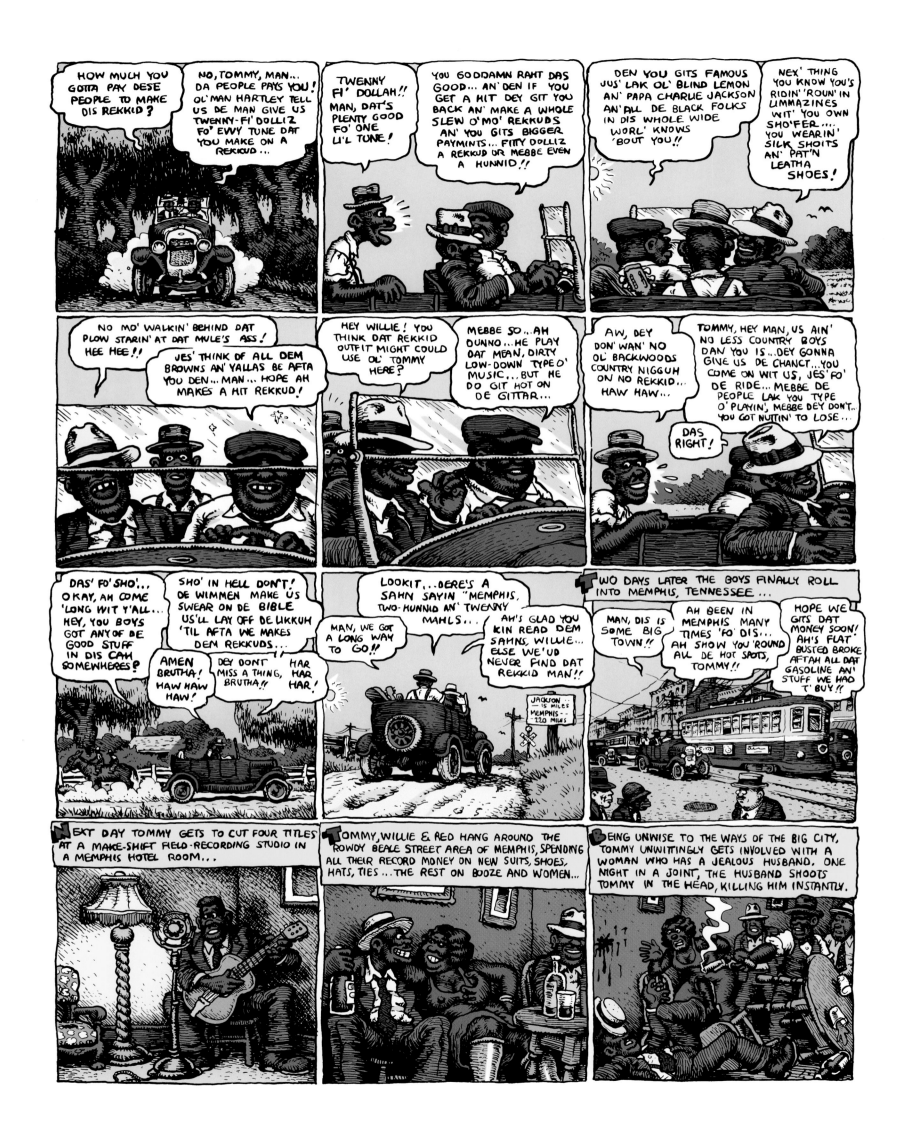

"Where Has It Gone, All the Beautiful Music of our Grandparents?" *Weirdo* #14, 1985

199

201

THEN CAME PROGRESS. LIFE GOT MORE COMPLICATED. THERE CAME EMPERORS, KINGS, QUEENS, PRINCES, POPES, DUKES, DUCHESSES AND SO ON. THESE ARISTOCRATS PUT HEAVY DEMANDS ON MUSICIANS. THEY WANTED SOOTHING, REFINED MUSIC AS BACKGROUND FOR THEIR ROMANTIC INTRIGUES, OR WHILE SCHEMING UP NEW WARS OF CONQUEST, OR BOTH...

MADAME, HOW AM I TO EXPRESS THE VIVIDNESS OF MY FEELINGS FOR YOU, IF ONLY TO COMPARE THIS GLOW IN MY HEART TO THAT WHICH I FELT ON THE GLORIOUS DAY WHEN MY MINISTERS CAME TO ME WITH THE JOYFUL NEWS THAT OUR GREAT ARMADA HAD SUCCESSFULLY LANDED AT CALAIS!?

SIR, YOUR WORDS ARE MOST ELOQUENT BUT YOUR SIMILE I FIND A BIT STRAINED,...KINDLY DO TRY AGAIN...

AT THE SAME TIME THE HUMBLE PEASANTS, THE POOR PEOPLE OF THE WORLD, STILL HAD THEIR LOW-DOWN FUNKY MUSIC. WHEN THESE PEOPLE GOT OFF WORK, THEY LIKED TO PARTY HARD,...THEY WOULD DANCE AND JUMP AROUND ALL NIGHT OR UNTIL THEIR NOSES BLED.

THINGS HAVEN'T CHANGED ALL THAT MUCH, YOU MIGHT SAY, BUT WAIT...THERE ARE SOME SUBTLE DIFFERENCES. MUSICIANS DIDN'T HAVE MICROPHONES OR AMPLIFIERS IN MEDIEVAL TIMES, SO THEY DIDN'T NEED ROAD MANAGERS TO HAUL THEIR EQUIPMENT AROUND FOR THEM. ALSO, THEY DIDN'T HAVE TO WORRY ABOUT VIDEO RIGHTS OR MERCHANDISING CLOUT, THINGS LIKE THAT.

SOME MUSICIANS IN OLDEN TIMES WERE DISREPUTABLE CHARACTERS WHO WANDERED FROM TOWN TO TOWN JUST LIKE NOW, BUT MOST WERE ORDINARY PEOPLE WHO HAD STRONG TIES TO THEIR FAMILY, VILLAGE, REGION...THEY PLAYED IN THE LOCAL STYLE, LEARNED FROM THEIR RELATIVES AND NEIGHBORS. COMMON PEOPLE OF THE LOWEST CLASSES SPOKE ON THEIR FIDDLES WITH A FIERCENESS AND BEAUTY THAT COULD MOVE AND EXCITE THE HEART AS DEEPLY AS ANY OFFICIAL "MASTERPIECE" BY MOZART OR BEETHOVEN *

* DON'T TAKE MY WORD FOR IT...LISTEN TO SOME OLD RECORDS PUT OUT ON REISSUE ALBUMS...

AND WHILE THE OLD WAYS OF PLAYING MUSIC (NOW CALLED "FOLK" MUSIC) DIDN'T CHANGE VERY MUCH OVER THE CENTURIES, THE ABSENCE OF FORMALISTIC RESTRICTIONS LEFT THE MUSICIANS A LOT OF FREEDOM TO EXPRESS THEIR OWN UNIQUENESS. THIS IS HOW IT WAS RIGHT UP TO OUR GRANDPARENTS' GENERATION!...AND THEN, AS MY DEAR OLD MOTHER ONCE TOLD ME ~

I REMEMBER BACK IN THE 'TWENTIES, MY MOTHER AND FATHER PLAYED MUSIC WITH THEIR FRIENDS ON WEEK-ENDS...OLD STRING-BAND MUSIC, Y'KNOW...... ON SUMMER EVENINGS THEY'D PLAY OUT ON THE FRONT PORCH.....

ALL UP AND DOWN OUR STREET ON TH' WEEK-ENDS YOU COULD HEAR THE PEOPLE PLAYING — BUT NONE OF US KIDS EVER PICKED UP AN INSTRUMENT... MY FATHER TRIED, BUT WE WEREN'T INTERESTED... WE LISTENED TO "OUR" MUSIC ON THE RADIO... ARTIE SHAW, BENNY GOODMAN,...WE WERE JITTERBUGS...THE STUFF OUR PARENTS PLAYED WAS STRICTLY CORNY TO US...WE WERE A BUNCH OF "HEP CATS"...

...WITH A HEY NONNY NONNY AND A HOT CHA CHA!

* WATERED DOWN NEGRO JIVE TALK

EVERYTHING IS CHANGING SO FAST..WHEN YOU'RE YOUNG YOU GOTTA BE HEP TO THE JIVE OR YOU'RE DOOMED.... TO BE "CORNY" IS TO BE A LOSER, OUT OF THE RUNNING, FINISHED, —BOOM! —KAPUT! THE KIDS WILL HAPPILY THROW THEIR PROUD HERITAGE ON THE GARBAGE HEAP IF IT MEANS BEING WITH IT, UP-TO-THE-MINUTE. THEY'LL SHIT-CAN IT EAGERLY, WITHOUT A MOMENT'S HESITATION, THEY "NEVER LOOK BACK."

HEY! GET SMART, YOU BUMPKIN!!

OH GOSH!

THIS PROCESS IS GOING ON ALL OVER THE WORLD TODAY, IN 1985...WHEREVER TECHNOLOGY INVADES A CULTURE, YOU FIND THE YOUTH EMBRACING IT, GOING FOR IT, DISDAINING THE OLD WAYS. THEY WANT THE GOODIES, THE SHINY TOYS, THE PROMISE OF ALL THAT GLITTER, THE COMFORT, THE CONVENIENCE, THE SOPHISTICATION—IT'S ONLY NATURAL!

ENVY OF EVERY KID IN THE VILLAGE

MENUDO

WELL, SO WHAT, YOU SAY? WHAT ARE THEY S'POSED TO DO, GO BACK AND SAY THEIR PRAYERS IN DIRT FLOOR HUTS?? WHAT'S WRONG WITH MODERN POP MUSIC? THEY'RE HAVING A GOOD TIME, WHAT TH' HELL'S THE DIFFERENCE? WHY ARE YOU IN SUCH A DITHER ABOUT IT ???

GRRR DIRTY OTA!!!

I DUNNO... I GUESS I GOT THIS WAY FROM LISTENING TO OLD RECORDS TOO MUCH...THESE ECHOES OF THE PAST... A LOST WORLD, TRUE ENOUGH...THE LOSS OF THESE RICH AND ANCIENT MUSICAL TRADITIONS...WELL, IT BREAKS MY FUCKIN' HEART!!

WHAT HAPPENED? WHAT HAPPENED TO THIS MUSIC??

AAH, YER SO FUCKIN' SENSITIVE!

ACTUALLY, ONE NIGHT RECENTLY I WAS SITTING IN THE BLUEBIRD NIGHTCLUB IN FORT WORTH, TEXAS, TAKING IN THE SCENE. I WAS KINDA "GETTING WITH" THE MUSIC—A MEXICAN BLUES BAND—TWO ELECTRIC GUITARS, ELECTRIC BASS, AND TWO SAXES—I WAS SORTA DIGGING IT.

WELL AWRIGHT!!

BUT AFTER AWHILE, I STARTED GETTING THAT OLD FEELING OF IRRITATION, AND THEN I ENDED UP VEXED, DIZGUSTED... WHY DOES IT HAVE TO BE SO GODDAMN LOUD?? IF THEY WERE PLAYING ACOUSTIC INSTRUMENTS, THE MUSIC WOULD SOUND SO MUCH BETTER! THIS ELECTRIC SHIT IS WAY OVERDONE—THAT'S A LOT OF WHAT IT COMES DOWN TO...

END

Aline Kominsky and
Robert Crumb, 1974-75

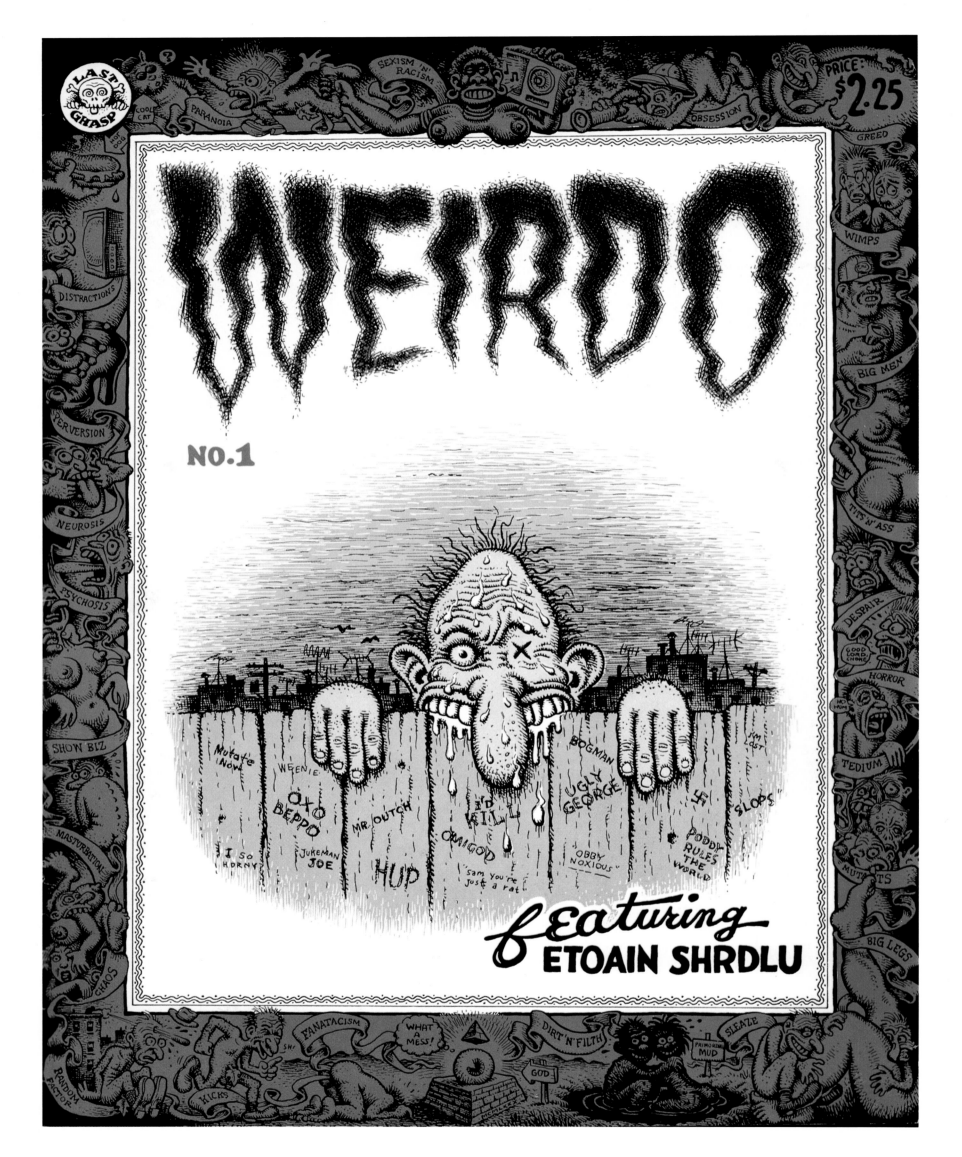

# "MY HIGH SCHOOL ART TEACHER DIDN'T LIKE ME. HE SAID 'IF YOU KEEP DOING THOSE CARTOONS, YOU'LL WIND UP SELLING PENCILS ON THE STREET!'"

WHEN I WAS 15, I VISITED STAN LYNDE, THE ARTIST WHO WROTE AND DREW THE COMIC STRIP *RICK O'SHAY*. HE SHOWED ME HOW HE WORKED. I WAS JUST SHOCKED AT HOW DIFFICULT THE PRODUCTION OF A PROFESSIONAL COMIC STRIP WAS. THERE WAS AN EXTRAORDINARY AMOUNT OF PREPARATION AND PLANNING. LYNDE ALWAYS DID VERY CAREFUL PRELIMINARY SKETCHES AND LAYOUTS FOR THE STRIP. HE HAD SOME OTHER GUY DOING THE LETTERING. INCREDIBLE! I COULDN'T BELIEVE THE AMOUNT OF TEDIOUS LABOR. IT WAS REALLY VERY DISCOURAGING TO ME. I GAVE UP THOUGHTS OF BEING A PROFESSIONAL CARTOONIST, BUT I HAD SUCH MOMENTUM FOR DRAWING COMICS, I JUST KEPT DOING IT. I HAD NO EXPECTATIONS ABOUT EVER BEING PUBLISHED BECAUSE MY WORK WAS JUST TOO LOOSE AND SLOPPY COMPARED TO THE STANDARDS OF THE TIME. IT AMAZED ME LATER WHEN *FRITZ THE CAT* WAS PUBLISHED. I DON'T THINK I EVEN PENCILED ANY OF THAT STUFF. I JUST DREW IT STRAIGHT OUT.

IN 1972, I WAS VISITING JAY LYNCH IN CHICAGO, AND ONE DAY HE SAID, "LET'S GO VISIT CHESTER GOULD AND TAKE SOME OF OUR WORK AND SEE WHAT HE THINKS OF IT." I BARELY BELIEVED THAT CHESTER GOULD WAS A REAL PERSON, MUCH LESS STILL DRAWING *DICK TRACY*. BACK IN 1955-56, CHARLES, MYSELF AND MAXON WERE HEAVILY INTO *DICK TRACY* AND FOR A TIME WE ALL STARTED DRAWING LIKE CHESTER GOULD. IT WAS THE ONLY STRIP I EVER CLIPPED OUT OF THE NEWSPAPER AND SAVED FOR A WHILE DURING THIS JOE PERIOD—FLATTOP JR. SEQUENCE. *DICK TRACY* HAD NEVER DECLINED. I ALWAYS THOUGHT IT WAS AS GOOD AT THE END AS IT WAS IN THE BEGINNING. MAYBE EVEN BETTER.

SO JAY AND I WENT DOWNTOWN TO THE CHICAGO TRIBUNE BUILDING AND WENT TO THE INFORMATION DESK. JAY HAD CALLED AHEAD AND MADE AN APPOINTMENT. WE WERE TOLD TO TAKE THE ELEVATOR TO THE TOP FLOOR OF THE TOWER AND THEN TAKE THE STAIRS. WE GOT TO THE TOP, AND IT WAS ALL ART DECO LIKE A SET OUT OF A MOVIE. WE TOOK THIS SPIRAL STAIRCASE UP AND CAME INTO A DOME-SHAPED ROOM WITH THE TOPS OF THESE ARCHED WINDOWS. BIZARRE! THERE WAS A GUY STANDING THERE SMOKING A CIGAR WHO LOOKED LIKE A JANITOR OR SOMETHING. HE SAID, "CAN I HELP YOU BOYS WITH SOMETHING?" WE TOLD HIM WE WERE LOOKING FOR CHESTER GOULD. THE GUY SAID, "I'M HIM." SO WE SHOWED HIM OUR WORK. HE FLIPPED THROUGH IT. HE DIDN'T READ IT, BUT HE LIKED THE FACT THAT OUR ARTWORK WAS DETAILED

AND SAID, "IT'S GOOD TO SEE THAT YOU YOUNG GUYS ARE GETTING INTERESTED IN DRAWING AGAIN! A LOT OF THESE MODERN CARTOONISTS HAVE THIS "QUICKY STYLE!" HE TALKED ABOUT THE COMIC STRIP BUSINESS A LITTLE BIT, BUT THEN HE STARTED RANTING ABOUT THE PRESENT STATE OF AMERICA, THE INCREASE IN CRIME, THAT WE HAVE TO CRACK DOWN MORE ON CRIMINALS AND HOW DANGEROUS IT WAS TO WALK THE STREETS OF CHICAGO.

GOULD PROBABLY SPENT A LOT OF TIME LOOKING DOWN ON THE STREETS OF CHICAGO FROM THOSE WINDOWS IN THE TRIBUNE TOWER. AT ONE POINT, HE LOOKED DOWN AND SPIED SOME RIFF-RAFF HANGING AROUND A PARKED CAR.

"PUNKS!" HE SAID. "IF THEY TRIED TO BREAK INTO MY CAR, I'D SET 'EM ON FIRE!" HE WAS REALLY CRAZY, BUT THAT WAS PART OF WHAT MADE *DICK TRACY* A VERY INTERESTING STRIP AND WHY HE WAS ABLE TO DO IT ALL THOSE YEARS AND MAINTAIN A HIGH LEVEL OF QUALITY. HE WAS A "LUMA-KICK," AS POPEYE WOULD SAY.

THE ONLY OLDER ARTIST OR WRITER WHOM I ADMIRED AND THEN ACTUALLY GOT TO KNOW WAS HARVEY KURTZMAN. GOD LOVE 'IM ... IT AMAZES ME TO THINK HOW AS A YOUNG PUNK OF 20 I WAS ABLE TO CONNECT WITH KURTZMAN. HE BECAME A VERY IMPORTANT PART OF MY LIFE. I NEVER GOT OVER IT. I WAS ALWAYS THRILLED TO BE IN HIS PRESENCE.

KURTZMAN WAS ALSO ONE OF THE FEW CARTOONISTS FROM HIS GENERATION WHO WAS CURIOUS AND INTERESTED IN THE UNDERGROUND COMIX SCENE. IT WAS ALIEN TO OLDER CARTOONISTS WHO SORT OF LOOKED AT IT WITH CONDESCENDING BEMUSEMENT. WHEN I SHOWED KURTZMAN MY LSD-INSPIRED CARTOONS, HIS FIRST REACTION WAS THAT THEY WERE VASTLY INFERIOR TO MY EARLIER STUFF. HE REALLY GAVE ME A DRESSING DOWN ABOUT IT. HE JUST DIDN'T GET IT. ALSO, KURTZMAN USED TO TELL ME I WAS "SABOTAGING" MY OWN SUCCESS. FROM HIS POINT OF VIEW, IF YOU GOT OFFERS FROM *PLAYBOY* OR HOLLYWOOD, YOU DID *NOT* TURN THEM DOWN. I TURNED DOWN AN OFFER TO DO A RECORD ALBUM COVER FOR THE ROLLING STONES BECAUSE I NOT ONLY HATED THEIR MUSIC, BUT ALSO THE ONLY THING COOLER THAN DOING A COVER FOR THE STONES WAS *NOT* DOING A COVER FOR THE STONES ... WHAT A FOOL, NOW THAT I THINK ABOUT IT. OH MAN, THE YOUNG HIPPIE CHICKS I COULD HAVE HAD WITH A STONES COVER UNDER MY BELT! OH, WELL! I WAS VERY PROTECTIVE OF MY CREATIVE INTEGRITY, ALWAYS. KURTZMAN DIDN'T UNDERSTAND THAT SO CLEARLY. BUT, YOU KNOW, HE WAS WORKING IN A VERY COMMERCIALLY CONSTRAINED ENVIRONMENT. THAT WAS HIS WORLD! MY ATTITUDE VEXED HIM BECAUSE HE WAS THRILLED TO GET OFFERS THAT PUT YOU ON THE MAP. THEN YOU COULD START TO COMMAND REALLY BIG BUCKS FOR YOUR WORK. BUT BEING A PART OF THE HIPPIE CULTURE, THE *PLAYBOY* SCENE JUST SEEMED LIKE A BIG JOKE TO ME, A LOT OF "STRAIGHT" BOOSHWAH NONSENSE. I WANTED NO PART OF IT.

*opposite*, cover, *Weirdo* no. 1, 1981; *above*, sketchbook detail, mid '70s

sketchbook page, 1975

STILL LIFE EXERCISE - FEB. 24TH '83

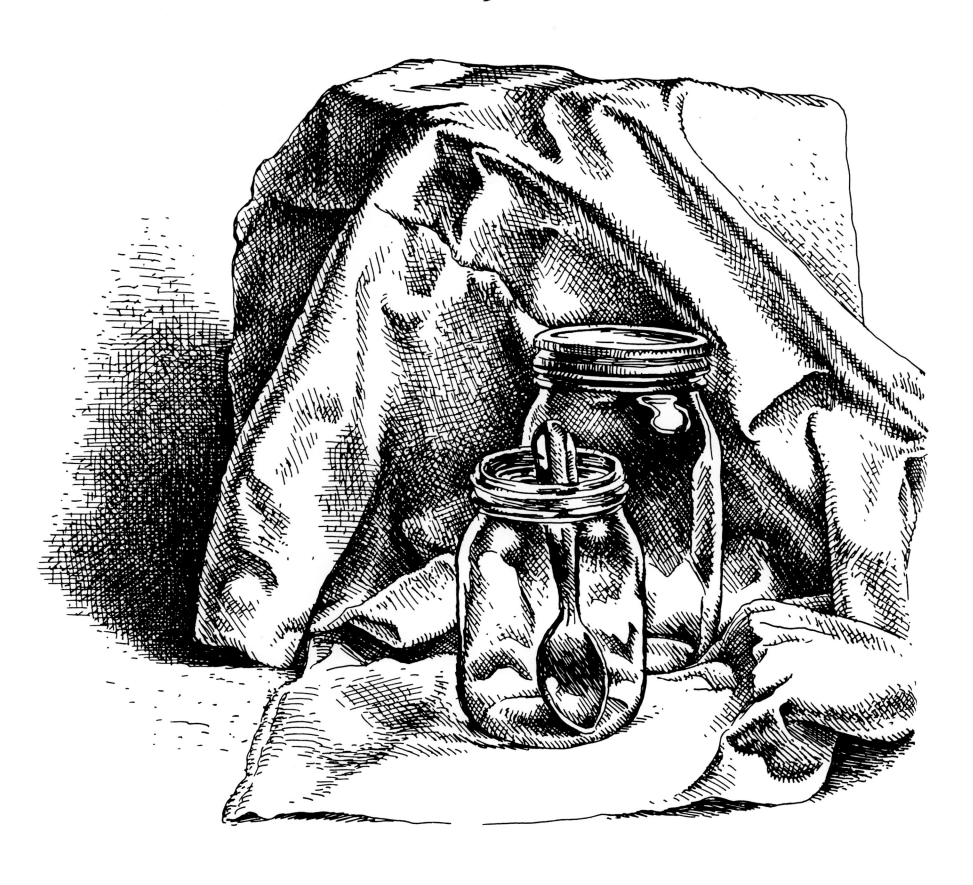

WOODPILE — DEC. 1ST '78

...and now, it's back to this stoopid Rapidographo....
actually it's a "Refograph"....

CHICKEN HOUSE
OCTOBER 1982

THE "VIEW"

R. CRUMB
NOVEMBER 16TH '82

# A NICE QUIET EVENING AT HOME ALONE...

"OPTICAL TRUTHS"

sketchbook page, early '90s

PLACE du DOYEN GACHON                    R. CRUMB '91

*Vues de Sauve* portfolio, 1991

PATH
IN THE "MER DES ROCHERS"
ABOVE SAUVE
SEPT. 30th, '96

215

# GETTING AWAY FROM PEOPLE...
## MUST BE BACK BY APERITIF TIME...

THE DEEP DARK PLACES
in the
"MER DES ROCHERS"
OCT. 11th '96

sketchbook page, early '80s

*opposite, Aline in
a Cubist Nightmare,
oil on canvas, 1980*

# Problems In Composition

It's too tight!

sketchbook page, early '80s

*opposite, Oy Oy Oydle–Oil Painting #1,
or Blue Man–Green Man,* oil on
canvas. 1980

opposite, *The Green Aline*, oil on canvas. 1980

224

*opposite,* sketchbook
*this page,* ***The Vulture***
bondo and lacquer. L

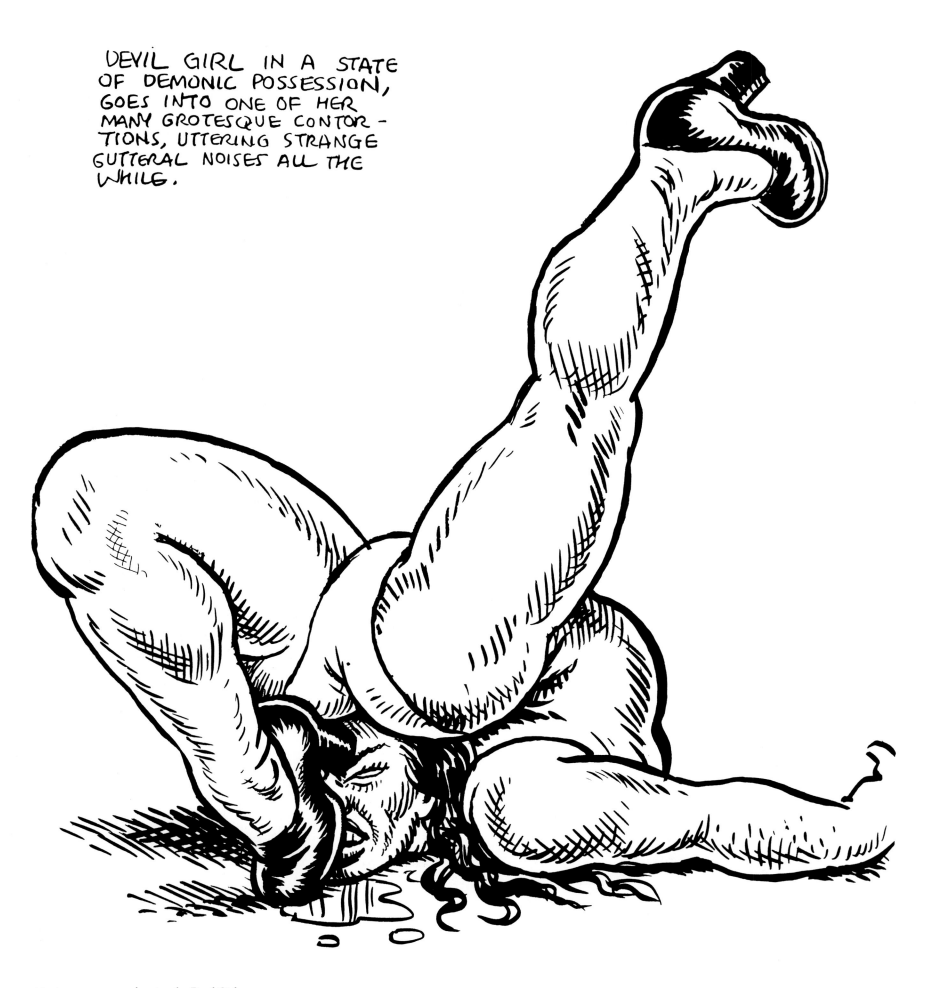

DEVIL GIRL IN A STATE OF DEMONIC POSSESSION, GOES INTO ONE OF HER MANY GROTESQUE CONTORTIONS, UTTERING STRANGE GUTTERAL NOISES ALL THE WHILE.

*opposite*, preparatory drawing for *Devil Girl*, 1995; *this page*, Devil Girl sketch, 1986

JUST BEFORE I STARTED **WEIRDO** IN 1980, ALINE WAS DOING SOME OIL PAINTINGS. THE SMELL OF THE PAINT AND TURPENTINE WAS VERY APPEALING, SO I THOUGHT I'D TRY IT. I HADN'T MESSED WITH OIL PAINT SINCE HIGH SCHOOL. ALINE GAVE ME SOME TIPS ON HOW TO USE PAINT, AND I GUESS I DID FIVE OR SIX PAINTINGS. BUT I RE-ALIZED THAT TO GET ANYTHING INTERESTING TAKES A LOT OF TIME.

I WAS INSPIRED TO MAKE A LIFE-SIZE FIGURE OF ONE OF MY FEMALE CHARACTERS IN 1989. SOME NEIGHBORS OF OURS IN WINTERS, CALI-FORNIA, HAD THIS BIG WOODEN FIGURE, LIFE-SIZE, IN THEIR LIVING ROOM THAT A FRIEND OF THEIRS MADE. I THOUGHT IT WOULD BE FUN TO MAKE SOME KIND OF WOODEN FIGURE WITH THIS SCULPTOR. HE DID MOST OF THE WOODWORK, AND I DID THE DETAILS. IT WAS A LOT OF WORK BUT CAME OUT SORT OF GOOD. I HAD AN ART SHOW IN SAN FRANCISCO IN 1990, AND I TOOK THE VULTURE GOD-DESS (I HAD ONLY FINISHED IT THE DAY BEFORE!) AND SET IT UP. IT SOLD THE SAME DAY! EVERYBODY STARTED SAYING, "YOU SHOULD MAKE ANOTHER STATUE SOMETIME!" THEN WE MOVED TO FRANCE. FIVE YEARS GO BY. I WAS THINKING ABOUT DOING AN-OTHER LIFE-SIZE SCULPTURE. SOMETHING IN ME WANTED TO DO THIS CRAZY POSE THAT I HAD MADE IN MY SKETCHBOOK: DEVIL GIRL IN A STATE OF DEMONIC POSSESSION. A FRIEND OF MINE, ALAIN SCHONS, SUGGESTED A WOODWORKER FRIEND OF HIS, YVES ROUANET. I TALKED TO HIM. YEAH, HE'S GAME TO DO IT. SO I MADE A BUNCH OF DRAW-INGS. ALAIN AND YVES SPENT A MONTH WORKING UP THE LIFE-SIZE WOODEN FIGURE, AND THEN I PROCEEDED TO WORK FOR FOUR MONTHS REWORKING AND DEVELOPING THE DETAILS. JEEZIZ, THAT WAS A LOT OF WORK! IT WAS FUN, THOUGH. I WAS THRILLED WHEN THE FORM AND THE DETAILS CAME TOGETHER THE WAY I WANTED THEM TO. THE DEVIL GIRL WAS COMING TO LIFE TO ME, I STARTED GETTING SEXUALLY EXCITED BY IT. THE DEVIL GIRL SCULP-TURE IS VERY POLITICALLY INCORRECT FOR THE ART MARKET. THE ART MAR-KET IS VERY POLITICALLY CORRECT RIGHT NOW, AND HERE I AM, A WHITE MALE, HETEROSEXUAL (I GOT THAT AGAINST ME), BAD! SO I MAKE THIS SCULPTURE. IT'S REALISTIC, IT'S FEMALE ... IN A SOMEWHAT DEGRAD-ING POSITION. I DUNNO ...

R. CRUMB '95

227

*opposite*,
*Devil Girl*,
wood, bondo
and lacquer.
Roughly life-
size, 1995;
*above, Devil
Girl*, side view;
*left*, preparatory
drawings for
*Devil Girl*, 1995

R. CRUMB '95

229

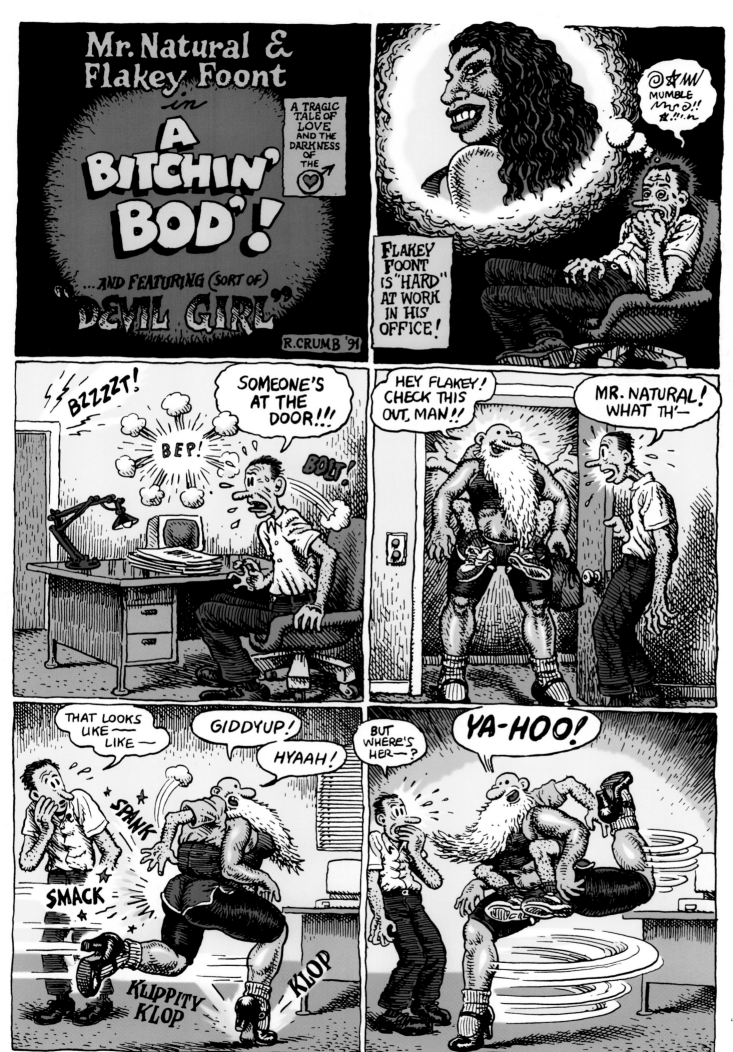

"A Bitchin' Bod," *Hup* no. 4, 1992

*opposite*, *Devil Girl* detail

232

233

234

235

236

237

239

242

243

"Burned Out Again!" sketchbook, 1990

245

# "DO I THINK OF MYSELF AS AN ENTERTAINER? YEAH...
## YA GOTTA AMUSE 'EM OR YOU'LL LOSE 'EM! TA HA!"

**B**UT I DON'T WANT TO BE JUST AN ENTERTAINER— I WANT TO TELL THE TRUTH, TOO! IN THE EARLY DAYS OF UNDERGROUND COMICS, I WAS SOMETIMES JUST A WISEASS WHO WANTED TO USE TRADITIONAL COMIC BOOK TECHNIQUES TO DO SHOCKING THINGS. FIRST, YOU HAVE TO SHOCK YOURSELF: "OH MY GOD! I'M REALLY BREAKING THROUGH MY INHIBITIONS HERE!" HEY, I WAS RAISED CATHOLIC IN FIFTIES AMERICA, WHICH WAS VERY, VERY SQUARE, SO PART OF WHAT WAS HAPPENING ALL THROUGH THE SIXTIES WAS BREAKING DOWN THAT STUFF, SEEING WHAT'S BEHIND IT AND TRYING TO FIGURE OUT WHERE TO GO AFTER THAT. THEN WHAT? CIVILIZATION MUST GO ON! WE DON'T WANT TO BECOME BARBARIANS OVER HERE! TO SORT IT ALL OUT IS COMPLICATED.

AS FAR AS VISUAL ART GOES, IT HAS TO REVEAL SOMETHING ABOUT REALITY THAT YOU CAN'T REALLY PUT INTO WORDS. ANY ARTIST WHO CAN EXPLAIN HIS WORK WITH WORDS IS NOT EXACTLY ON THE RIGHT TRACK. IT'S TOUGH. YOU'RE ALWAYS PROBING DOWN IN THE DARK AND YOU REVEAL THINGS TO YOURSELF AS YOU DO YOUR ART. PEOPLE WHO USE FORMULAS OR USE THEIR SKILL MAINLY JUST TO MAKE MONEY— I DON'T KNOW HOW THEY CAN STAND IT. IT MUST BECOME VERY BORING, I WOULD THINK.

**C**OMICS HAVE THEIR OWN SPECIAL TAKE ON REALITY. THERE ARE MANY DIFFERENT APPROACHES TO COMICS, BUT IT DOESN'T DO WHAT LITERATURE CAN DO. COMICS ARE DIFFERENT, AND WHEN CARTOONISTS TRY TO "ELEVATE" THE FORM, SO TO SPEAK, IT'S IN DANGER OF BECOMING PRETENTIOUS. COMICS HAVE ALWAYS LENT THEMSELVES TO THE LURID AND SENSATIONAL, STARTING AS FAR BACK AS PENNY PRINTS OF THE MARTYRDOM OF THE SAINTS OR BATTLE SCENES IN THE 1500s. THE PICTURES HAVE TO BE STRONG. YOU CAN GET VERY PERSONAL WITH COMICS, BUT TO IMBUE COMICS WITH SERIOUS LITERARY SUBTLETY SEEMS ABSURD TO ME. THERE'S SOMETHING ROUGH AND WORKING CLASS ABOUT COMICS. IF YOU GET TOO FAR AWAY FROM THAT, WELL, IT CAN TURN SILLY ON YOU.

**I** CAN'T READ A LOT OF THE HEAVY, SERIOUS COMICS PEOPLE ARE DOING NOW. THEY STRIKE ME AS RATHER PRETENTIOUS SOMETIMES. "YOU READ IT — I CAN'T." WHEN I THINK ABOUT TRYING TO APPLY MY ARTISTIC SKILLS TO SHOWING HOW SOME PROTOTYPICAL PERSON'S DEEP INNER PSYCHE WORKS, AND HOW THEY INTERACT WITH THE WORLD, AS IN FLAUBERT'S GREAT NOVEL *MADAME BOVARY,* THE VERY THOUGHT MAKES ME FEEL TIRED, DRAINED ... WHEW!

**M**Y APPROACH TO COMICS HAS ALWAYS BEEN SOMEWHAT SPONTANEOUS. I'M USUALLY ONLY A FEW PANELS AHEAD— I DON'T LIKE TO PLAN IT OUT TOO MUCH. OTHERWISE THE LABOR INVOLVED IN THE DRAWING BECOMES BORING, TEDIOUS. I JUST CAN'T DO IT. IT'S NOT IN ME ... MAYBE I'M LAZY ... SO BE IT ... I KIND OF RESOLVE THE STORY IN MY MIND AS I DRAW. I USE THE OLD COMIC-STRIP STEREOTYPES TO REVEAL MYSELF TO MYSELF. I'M BOTH MR. NATURAL AND FLAKEY FOONT. I'M ALSO MR. SNOID ... ALL THOSE SNOID CHARACTERS. THAT'S EASIER FOR ME THAN TRYING TO CREATE AN ELABORATE LITERARY CONSTRUCT. I COULDN'T DO IT!

**I**'VE ALWAYS CARRIED AROUND A SKETCHBOOK AND WOULD PUT DOWN ANY IDEAS THAT CAME INTO MY HEAD FOR POSSIBLE FUTURE USE IN THE COMICS. THESE SKETCHBOOKS BECAME MORE AND MORE LIKE PRIVATE DIARIES AS TIME WENT ON, AND OF COURSE, I'D GET NERVOUS WHEN SOMEONE WOULD SAY, "HEY, LET ME LOOK AT YOUR SKETCHBOOK!" IT BECAME PROBLEMATIC CARRYING IT AROUND BECAUSE AFTER I GOT FAMOUS, EVERYBODY WANTED TO LOOK AT IT. FOR A WHILE, I TRIED TO KEEP SEPARATE BOOKS, A "SECRET" SKETCHBOOK AND A "PUBLIC" SKETCHBOOK, BUT THAT BECAME TOO CUMBERSOME. I WOULD GET INSPIRED TO DO SOMETHING SECRET AND PRIVATE WHEN I WAS OUT IN THE WORLD WITH MY "PUBLIC" SKETCHBOOK. OH, BOY ... AND NOW THAT MY SKETCHBOOKS HAVE BEEN PUBLISHED, IT IS NO LONGER EASY FOR ME TO CASUALLY PICK IT UP AND DOODLE IN IT. EVERY PAGE HAS TO BE A MASTERPIECE. EVERYTHING I DO NOW IS FOR PUBLICATION—EVEN IF I DRAW ON THOSE PLACEMATS IN RESTAURANTS. IT BECOMES ALMOST IMPOSSIBLE TO BE SPONTANEOUS WITH THE OLD RAPIDOGRAPH ANYMORE. I TEND TO DRAW IN THE SKETCHBOOK MORE WHEN I'M ON THE ROAD TRAVELING, OR IF I'M IN A PERIOD OF DEPRESSION. THE PROBLEM IS THAT I DON'T GET AS DEPRESSED AS MUCH AS I USED TO. DURING THOSE PERIODS WHEN I FELT CONFUSED AND VEXED, I'D PICK UP MY SKETCHBOOK AND DRAW A VEXED-LOOKING CHARACTER ON THE PAGE. I GO BACK AND FORTH, TAPPING INTO MY LSD-INSPIRED INNER VISION, OR IF THAT FAILS ONE CAN ALWAYS SIMPLY OPEN ONE'S EYES AND DRAW REALITY. DRAW FROM LIFE ... DRAW ANYTHING... THE FIRST THING THAT COMES INTO YOUR HEAD OR THE FIRST THING THAT CATCHES YOUR EYE. SOMETIMES I WOULD START WITH MY OWN RIGHT HAND OR THE FOLDS OF MY PANT LEG. I HAVE NEVER DEVELOPED A SURE, FAST LINE. I DON'T HAVE IT IN ME. MY LINE QUALITY IS QUIVERY, NEUROTIC AND UNCERTAIN, WHICH, HIDDEN UNDER A LOT OF CROSS-HATCHING, WORKS. CROSS-HATCHING CAN COVER UP A LOT OF WEAKNESSES ... AND WITH A LIBERAL USE OF WHITE-OUT, THERE YOU HAVE IT!

*opposite,* unpublished cover, 1979; *above,* sketchbook detail, 1991

247

EDITOR, ART DIRECTOR, AND COLORIST
Peter Poplaski

PUBLISHER
Denis Kitchen

ASSOCIATE EDITOR
Robert Boyd

DESIGNERS
Lisa Stone-Mutti and Amie Brockway

PRODUCTION ASSISTANTS
Evan Metcalf, Ali Karasic, Peter Lohman, Chris Shadoian

ASSISTANT COLORISTS
Chris Shadoian, "Squinty" Rotunda, Agathe Couderes

COLOR SEPARATIONS
Digital Chameleon

PROOFREADER
Ina Iansiti

Photo credits: p. ii—Lora Fountain; p. 48—Terry Gilliam; pp. 130, 218, 249—Gregg Gannon; p.138 (top)—Suzanne Williams; p. 221—Neal Halfon; p. 222—Malcolm Whyte; pp. 228-230—Claude Simon



Special thanks to the following people: Aline Kominsky-Crumb, Adele Kurtzman, Charles Boucher, Eric Sack, Alexander Acevedo, Hilary Bangash and the Alexander Gallery in New York, Paul Harrington, N.C. Christopher Couch, "Squinty" Rotunda, Judy Hansen, Lora Fountain, Michael Pietsch and Denis Kitchen.

PETER POPLASKI is a designer, painter, editor and cartoonist. He has colored and designed many comics and books including *The Spirit, Male Call, Steve Canyon* and classic reprints of *Batman, Superman* and *Zorro*. He lives in France, where he paints and fences.

# WELL, GOD, WHATAYA THINK?
## HOW DID I GET TO BE SUCH A
# DAMN FOOL?!